7/27/01

George E. Decker

Charles:
"Now that you are getting into management, training & leader-ship" I thought you might like George's ideas in his book. He & I "treadmill" together & talk about these things. Casey Stengel's quote is apro- (next 2 pages) pos to the team concept which I was brought up in since H/S.

Sounds like you have an excellent position & are being trained in the technical aspects. Good luck.
Grandad Charlie,   7/27/01
Gaithersburg,
md.

GETTING PEOPLE TO WORK TOGETHER EFFECTIVELY

GEORGE C. BODDIGER

American Literary Press, Inc.
Five Star Special Edition
Baltimore, Maryland

GETTING PEOPLE TO WORK TOGETHER EFFECTIVELY

Library of Congress
Cataloging in Publication Data
ISBN 1-56167-548-2

Library of Congress Card Catalog Number:
99-66205

Published by

American Literary Press, Inc.
Five Star Special Edition
8019 Belair Road, Suite 10
Baltimore, Maryland 21236

Manufactured in the United States of America

It's easy to get the players.
Getting 'em to play together, that's the hard part.

—Casey Stengel

CONTENTS

Contents (continued)

CHART LOCATIONS

Introduction

No one is prepared for his promotion to supervisor. But where do you turn?

This book is intended to be the source reference for first line supervisors to turn to when they have questions about how they should handle their new tasks.

Your first step into supervision is usually into what is called "first line supervision," which means the supervision of workers who do essentially the basic functions of the enterprise.

Normally, workers in these units are beginners who have never worker full-time before, or who have difficulty progressing into more complicated positions.

Your title may be almost anything, including owner, but if you direct the work of people who handle the fundamental tasks of the business, you are a first line supervisor. In this book, I will use the title "supervisor" to identify the position of administering the basic work of the company.

Either men or women can be first line supervisors. Since the English language seems not yet to have identified one word meaning either he or she, or him or her; for ease of reference I've used he or him. A choice had to be made to avoid clumsy references and be grammatically as correct as possible.

It is also important to use one term to indicate the organization where the base unit exists. I have selected "company" simply because it eliminated trying to qualify each time whether the reference is to a store, factory, law firm, corporation, etc. The principles are the same, anyway.

There is no pretence in this work that the suggestions set forth are intellectually brilliant, nor do they create frontiers of new knowledge. The ideas presented have been distilled from more than 43 years of varied business experience, including nearly 40 years of supervisory responsibilities starting with a unit of three people and at various times including as many as

2,000. For 24 years, I was at different times chief executive officer of three life insurance companies where I was responsible for the total operations of each organization.

What appears here is the essence of those years of experience from a practical standpoint of what can actually be used by a first line supervisor. Many ideas are very simple. But they are also effective, and have been used successfully by working supervisors.

The practices cited here have come from all types of businesses, volunteer groups, and some academic organizations. What has been included is what I believe to be the best actions I've seen; from a viewpoint of simplicity, ease of adoption, and effectiveness. Undoubtedly, there are others that will work— but I know the ones here can work.

Management theory will inevitably be exposed in the development of ideas. The objective of this book, however, is to provide the beginning supervisor with a practical guide that can serve as a reference point when he is faced with supervisory problems. Written, we hope, in an easily understandable manner, the ideas can then be readily applied to most of the routine problems of first line supervisors.

Productivity of all organizations is currently a major concern of businesses worldwide. In truth, increased productivity has always been the major source of growth in the world. Only by producing more from the same combinations of labor, capital, and management will the lives of people improve.

The base from which improved productivity can be achieved most effectively are the primary units of the organization. If these function well, total results will be generally good. If these function poorly, there is no way for the whole organization to be effective.

It's said that an army is as good as its corporals. If so, a business is as good as it's first line supervisors.

Charts and work sheets in this work have been portrayed in simple form so as to apply in any circumstances, but may be committed to computers for ease of handling, if one is available.

So many people have contributed over the years to the ideas presented here that there is no way proper credit can be given to all of them. Suffice, perhaps, that everyone who touches another's life has an impact. The sum total of this becomes "you"—your feelings and beliefs—as you've weighed and judged experiences, observations, opinions, and desires of yourself and others.

It is impossible to repay those who have helped me. By giving to others the best of what has happened to me, is my only method of repaying those who so mightily have helped me. This book may do that. I hope it does.

Chapter 1

You Are Now the "Boss"

You've always wanted to be the boss—and here you are. But now what?

To yourself, you haven't changed. To your new subordinates, however, your entire role has switched. If you were a co-worker before, you are now different—you're the boss. If you came from outside the unit, you may have the advantage of starting with this group as the boss—but you are not just a fellow-worker.

As a supervisor, it is your responsibility to get production from your unit—not to do the production work yourself. As a good worker, you have been accustomed to producing a good volume of output and the temptation as a supervisor is to try to do all the unit's work yourself. You can't, and you shouldn't try.

Your job now as the supervisor is to get your workers to produce as you want them to. This is a much harder job than doing production work yourself.

Remember, a good supervisor must be just a little "lazy" so he really doesn't want to do all the work himself, but delegates the productive activities to his workers—and then watches to see that the work gets done, or finds out ways to get it done.

People vary widely in physical characteristics, mental abilities and desire drive. You must now identify those qualities needed on the job assigned to each worker and the worker's characteristics, abilities, and desires. When there is a fit between the job and the worker, productive output will result. Simply, your job is to identify, or develop, the fit.

In supervision, you must face reality. Things are not always the way they should be—or the way you want them to be—but that's the way they are. You should be neither an optimist nor a pessimist, but a realist. Deal with people and events the way they are and your results will be the best possible under the true circumstances that exist at the moment.

You are not expected to be a reformer. You are a doer. Don't waste your time trying to make people over. Accept them as they are and try to fit them into your unit, building on their strengths and compensating for their weaknesses. (Everyone has some of both.)

In dealing with people it is well to keep in mind that there are indeed "bad boys". Refusing to accept this will be a cause of dismay in time. When you are sure you have a truly "bad boy", don't delay—get a replacement.

Most people want to do a worthwhile job. You are to help them achieve their objectives.

People do not work <u>for</u> you, they work <u>with</u> you—a distinct difference.

Many "types of people" will greet you as you start your new job:

The leaner—who immediately wants to get on your good side to ease his own possible future problems.

The outsider—he's not a member of the "in-group" in the unit and wants a friend—even the boss.

The stoolie—he'll try to earn your favor by reporting on the misdeeds of every one else.

The bragger—"see me do the best job of anyone here." If he actually does, he isn't a bragger, just an overloud and perhaps immature seeker of attention.

The quiet one—says little to anyone. Often ignored by the others—too quiet—which may or may not conceal a good worker.

The confident, self-assured one—hopefully truly confident and self-assured, because he's truly competent.

And all the other possible combinations of people.

Why are people so different? It makes the job getting things done so complicated?

It has always been so, which gives you a first insight into why supervisors are paid more than workers and why many fail in the job. You must deal with all kinds of people while still maintaining a steady flow of output. Tough job! But fascinating because it is constantly challenging and extremely satisfying to those who can do it well.

Another aspect of your new position is your effect on the people in your unit. You set the example for them to follow, whether you want to or not. Your workers will do what they see you do, and refrain from doing those things which you don't do—generally. You are a role model now. If you are on time to work—your workers usually will be on time; if you are cheerful and upbeat—your workers will tend to be cheerful and upbeat—and the opposite if you are the opposite. Demand high standards of performance from yourself, and your workers will do the same of themselves.

Be careful what you say. Your comments will be

interpreted by your workers, and often misinterpreted, so be pleasant but refrain from saying things that might be considered offensive. Think about the two psychiatrists who met and one of them said, "Good morning," and the other said, "I wonder what he meant by that?"

In recent years there has been much talk about "new" Japanese techniques of business organizations and operation centering around participation of workers in determining objectives and how their work is to be done. Actually, this practice has always been an integral part of effective worker performance in this country although recent emphasis has highlighted its successes.

While worker initiative and change is immensely valuable, as pointed out here, it complements the efforts of a good first line supervisor to make an operation run smoothly.

It is interesting that during the recent recession in Japan, there has been sudden action to recognize the importance of enlightened process direction by "team leaders" and supervisors. Blending of supervising skills, with workers help and support, as proposed in this book, continues to develop the best production results.

CHAPTER 2 ———————

WHERE DO YOU BEGIN?

First: Make a list of each of the people who will report to you.

Second: Obtain all the information you can find about them from existing files and contacts. A simple form like the one at the end of this chapter will help keep the data organized.

Third: Talk with each person. Tell him you'll make notes so you can remember important facts accurately. Start by verifying the information you already have. Get the other person to talk. Once started talking, most people will relax and volunteer information.

Fourth: Listen! To what's said and to what isn't said. Nod your head at appropriate times to indicate you are listening and understanding. It also encourages the talker to continue. Try not to talk yourself, and don't comment unfavorably on anything the other person says. Smile—it's encouraging. Notice such comments as "You wouldn't be interested in that," "That's not important," and similar. Follow up by saying, "Tell me about it anyway," or "Try me. I'll understand," or similar encouraging and non-judgemental comments. Your goal is to find out what is important to the other person. Once you know his feelings and ideas of what's important you can better understand why he does some things, or doesn't do them.

Fifth: Ask, "Why do you work here?" Listen carefully to the answer and then try to be sure you have the true reason. My father said years ago that there are two reasons for everything: The reason you give and the real reason.[1] Search until you feel you have the real reason. It will be invaluable to know that in the weeks and months ahead. If you run into resistance or any unfavorable reaction, stop and make a mental note to search for the real reason later. If it is difficult to find the real reason the person works with you, it probably means that it is extremely important and not easily spoken by the other person. This can be a sign to watch for in the future.

Sixth: Complete the talk (NOT an interview—interview has bad connotations to many people.) Purpose of this talk is to just get acquainted.

Seventh: Offer to tell something of your own history. Make it as long or short as your listener wishes. Watch for signs of indifference or lack of interest. When you see them—stop!

---

[1]It might be well at this time to use a technique suggested by Professor. Howard T. Lewis of the Harvard Business School when he took a new job as a purchasing agent. His comments to salesmen who called on him were: "I'm new in this position and you can fool me now. But if you do, I'll learn and in the future I'll remember those who fooled me in the beginning and you won't be able to fool me again." To some people this might be a valuable observation.

Prepare your reference sheet and put it into a three-ring binder so it is readily available but kept private and in a secure place. (Even, perhaps, at home so prying eyes won't see it—and make your entries each night when you get back to your home.)

Enter observations, actions, and reactions immediately after they occur (very important.) Such notes will reveal over a period of time a clearer picture of the other person. It will also tell you something about yourself. Look at your comments and see if the problem with this individual may be your own attitude towards him. Prejudices creep into notes over a period of time. Be sure you are frank in your comments—otherwise you'll lose the true value of your effort.

Keeping the record on each person is tiresome and time consuming but essential. You cannot keep all instances of observation for all your people in your mind. The tremendous hazard of doing so is that you will remember only some of the occasions—either especially good or exceptionally bad—and base a judgment on them rather than the whole picture. Also, you will tend to remember some people and not others. Your objective is to develop the most productive work force you can, not just the workers you like or who are constantly brought to your attention by their occasional unusual actions.

Record keeping time for you is productive time because it makes it possible for you to do the best job. Don't slight it.

CONFIDENTIAL
Personal Record

Name _____

Address _____

Home Phone Number _____

Spouse's Name _____

Spouse Work Outside Home? _____

Children

Name	Age	Activities (List specifics)

Goals & Desires _____

Position Held Here _____

Prior Positions Held _____

Education _____

OBSERVATIONS

Date	Formal (F) Informal (I)	Description

CHAPTER 3 ——————————

WHAT YOU SHOULD KNOW ABOUT PEOPLE

Most obvious: Every person is different from every other.
Next obvious: Every person is different at different times.
Next: To get anyone to do what you would like them to do,
  you must understand how he *is at that moment,* and can
  reasonably be expected to be in the immediate future.
Next: It is impossible to please all workers all the time and
  be an effective supervisor. You will at some time have
  to take an action that *someone* will dislike. Be prepared
  to accept it.

Recognizing these points suggest that the only true
techniques for being a supervisor are:

1. Know every worker in as great a depth as possible. The
   more you know about a person the better you understand
   his feelings and actions.
2. Keep in as close contact with each worker as possible so

you know his feelings as close as possible at all times (they change constantly so you must also be working at this constantly to understand what causes a worker to do what he does *at the time.*)
3. Don't meddle in another's personal life. You only want to understand his actions—not influence *nor criticize.*

<u>Understanding</u>

Broadly speaking, understanding each of your workers gives you a realization of why he works and how he works. Knowing these two factors will give you the needed insight to direct him in a productive way.

Benjamin M. Selekman, noted labor professor from the Harvard Business School, urged his students to remember a basic fact about all workers:

"People do not leave their personal problems at home when they come to work. They bring them along with them."

Too often this concept has been distorted to mean that prying into personal problems is desirable, or that knowledge of a personal problem means overlooking poor work, insubordination, or other unproductive attitudes.

No.

Professor Selekman's admonition means that an understanding of a worker's personal problems will help you to direct his activities in a way which will meet his current emotional needs.

For example: A worker shows up an hour late for work. Professor Selekman's approach would be to find out why:

"Overslept"

"Up all night with sick baby (wife)"

"Auto accident"

"Didn't feel like coming to work."

"Worked until midnight on your special project to get it done and then overslept."

etc . . . . . .

Understanding each of the explanations does nothing but make it possible to judge how best to treat this issue. For example:

"Overslept." Why? "Didn't set alarm or didn't hear alarm." You: "What do you plan to do, so this won't happen again?"

1. Nothing." You: "There is a need for everyone to be on time so all work can proceed as planned. Tardiness hurts the entire unit. If repeatedly tardy, it can affect compensation or cause you to be fired."

2. "Hide the alarm so I'll be sure to get up, or I'll have a friend call me on the phone, etc. . ." (Anything constructive. The first time this happens—O.K., You: "Try not to let it happen again." The second time—same comments as in 1 above.

"Up all night with sick baby (wife)"

1. Be *genuinely* interested in how things were at home when he left. Is there any help that can be arranged? (Does the company have a nurse service that can be dispatched to help? Is there a Visiting Nurses organization that can be contacted? Is there someone (your wife, sister, friend) who could be helpful? Should baby (wife) be sent to the hospital?

2. This situation is serious to the worker and to you. He will have his mind on his home problem. If there is a way to let him check on the situation at home from time to time (even a quick visit if distance permits)—do it. If this is not possible, *you* check, and let the worker know the status.

3. As a supervisor, you are still responsible for getting out the required work. You cannot just overlook the loss of one worker's efforts. Look around for

any other solutions. Redistribution of work, after explanation of the problem to the other workers; reschedule work for today but make it up tomorrow (with your boss' understanding); can you fill in for the worker for a time while he checks on the situation in his home?

4. Primarily, however, remember that you are responsible for your unit's output. Recognizing the needs of your workers is excellent. Finding a way to alleviate his distress is good, but the work must go on. Too often, supervisors sympathize with the worker's problem and accept absenteeism, poor work, or loss of production as the only solution to this situation. Don't do it.

Use your imagination and creativity to achieve a positive action to fulfill your responsibility and be aware of the worker's real home problem at the same time.

It is essentially a good rule to respond to all people problems by asking yourself, "If I were the other person, what would I believe would be the proper thing for my boss to do?"

In your position as a supervisor, you have assigned responsibilities which impact the above rule, since what you would like others to do to you refers to other supervisors in your same position. For instance, you may not like to have someone discharge you because of your continued sloppy work. But your supervisor would have to do so in order to fulfill his responsibilities if your performance required it.

It is well to remember that the circumstances involved at this time can affect what should be done.

Very important: Treating all people the same is *not* being fair. People should be treated the way they *deserve* to be treated. All people in the *same circumstances* should be treated the same.

For example: A worker with an excellent record and service of two years asks for a day off for a reason special to him. Assuming it is possible to do so, such a request should be granted. A worker with three weeks of service who has already been absent one day asks for a day off for the same reason. Request denied.

These two situations are different. Your response to the second worker is: "Sorry, you are needed here. (If he raises objections because the first worker is given the day off, your response is: "When you've been here two years with the same excellent record as the other worker and the same circumstances arise, you'll get the day off too."

People get treated the same when they are in the same circumstances.

You will probably find this approach being questioned, particularly by some younger workers. In some instances, those from the "me-too" generation expect everything to be given to them without regard to the treatment they may deserve. To agree to such a plea will cause you operational problems in your unit from the persons involved—and the rest of your workers.

You should also remember that your unconscious actions may create a feeling among your workers about you. Such little things as referring to the people in your unit as "my people" can be offensive to some. Use of a term like "fellow-workers," "associates," or "partners" or similar, may be more acceptable.

Along the same line, many people have a great tendency to overuse the word "I"—"I'll see this is done," "I'll do that," etc. Use of the term "we" when referring to your unit will give a better impression. "Our company," rather than "my company," gets a more favorable response.

<u>Appreciation</u>

In dealing with anyone, one of the most effective phrases is "Thank you." It never offends. It expresses appreciation and *everyone* likes to be appreciated.

Years ago in the military service, I worked in a supply depot. Part of my assignment involved my obtaining files from another section of the depot. About a month after I had been assigned there someone asked one of the file clerks if she had met the "new Lieutenant" yet. Her response, "You mean the one who always says 'Thank you?'" In an installation with 2,500 people, it was interesting to be identified in such a positive manner.

"Thank you" works even better with people who are not accustomed to being thanked. The words come as a pleasant surprise to them. It implies to people that you are aware of the value of their services. Since this ties in closely with each person's sense of importance, he responds favorably to someone who appears to recognize his worth.

Philosophy Professor William James commented years ago: The deepest principle of human nature is the craving to be appreciated. Remember this!

<u>Encouragement</u>

Most of us do not perform every task at our best. Some of your workers will not be able to accomplish their work with the degree of accuracy or speed that you believe is necessary. You are always faced with the mental question: Which gets the better results—screaming or quiet insistence on improvement?

No improvement will occur unless the worker himself does it. Your job is to know what method of encouragement to use, and at what time. Here is where your knowledge of your workers will serve you very well. If you've talked with the worker often and listened hard, you'll understand what method will work best with each person. It is a matter of knowing the people.

Thousands have ceased to try to do their best because they have been reminded only of their worst.

This is true even in schoolwork. Elementary-school children were tested with arithmetic problems. Those who had only mistakes pointed out improved 20 per cent in a week. The others, whose errors were overlooked and who were encouraged for the sums they had right, improved 70 per cent![2]

Most people do respond to words of encouragement sincerely spoken, along with worthwhile suggestions for improvement.

A most effective method of encouragement is to give credit when and where it is due. Do not try to take credit for a favorable event for yourself, when someone else was the originator, or contributor. Nothing will "turn off" new ideas and a spirit of cooperation like creating the image that you will "steal" all good ideas as your own. Be extra generous in passing out compliments for those who have done something worthwhile. There is what I call a *Human Relations Principle* which states: The more credit you give away; the more credit you get. This Principle works just as surely as any principle of physics. Try it!

People Hear What They Want to Hear

This characteristic is normal.

We all do it because we want to hear what agrees with our desires at the moment.

One way to avoid misunderstandings resulting from this trait is to ask the person to whom you make a statement to repeat it to you *as he understands* what you said. This approach then requires the listener to rephrase what he

---

[2] *The Technique of Handling People* by Donald A. Laird, McGraw-Hill, Inc.

thought he heard, into his own words, which should reflect his understanding of the discussion. He will also put the emphasis where he thinks it belongs in his understanding. If what he says agrees with what you intend—great. If not, you then have a chance to repeat the process until you are both clear on your meaning.

No one should object to this procedure for clarification.

The normal tendency is for the person giving the instructions to repeat them, usually in a louder voice, if the listener doesn't understand. This approach will not clarify the other person's understanding. It is better to require him to say it himself.

Irving J. Lee in a great little book entitled *How To Talk With People* (See Appendix 8) reminds everyone that every conversation is really three conversations:

1. What I said.
2. What I thought I said.
3. What *you* thought I said.

Understanding a conversation in this framework points out the difficulty in being sure that all three conversations are the same.

Words do not mean the same to all people. Your experience, education, background, and personality affect your concept of the meaning of a given word. People exposed to "street talk" understand it—those not in that environment don't. ("Cool" is good; "hot" is not, etc.)

You can use a similar approach in written communications to that described above by asking the recipient to write you a letter or memorandum of his understanding of your request. It requires the recipient to express his understanding of what he heard from you. It might very well be different—and you will never realize it by your simply referring to your original communication, or the recipient saying, "I've read your letter and I agree."

In a somewhat related manner, if you have a

conversation with someone, you both agree on the decision and you ask the other person to respond in writing, but suppose he doesn't? It is then very wise to send a letter or memorandum to that person saying what you believe to be the agreement, and ask him to reply if your understanding disagrees with his. At least, then, if a disagreement arises later, you've presented your understanding at the time in writing and given him a chance to object if your position is different from his belief. It is difficult for the other person to object later, when he didn't do so upon getting your original letter or memo.

It is easier to "hear" good news than bad. A compliment will be savored right past a later sentence that concerns something less desirable. Most of us do not like to emphasize the unpleasant, so it often is put less positively than the pleasant—and thereby goes "unheard" by the listener. Careful repetition of the less desirable parts of a conversation can oftentimes keep it from getting lost in the general flow of talk.

Some sources of good supervisory practice have said that reprimand or disciplinary comments should always be accompanied by saying something good about the person involved. This concept is related to the real concern that some people are devastated by criticism and should be figuratively supported by something nice. It is also related to the concept that you should not destroy hope in a person.

It seems practical to follow a plan, then, of giving criticism first in the conversation and closing with some favorable comment. If the action is a stern one, such as a final warning on performance which may result in termination if not corrected, the impact may be softened too much by such an approach. It is often much better to be firm in the reprimand. Then follow-up *at a later time* with some favorable comment, if possible. Do this the same day.

An old proverb is: "Never let the sun go down on a

disagreement." Not letting the sun go down without a reassuring word after a reprimand is also a good practice.

Understanding your workers is essential when talking to them about mistakes or need for improvement. People respond differently to such conversations. Great leaders of men throughout history have known when to praise and when to punish. It is said that General George S. Patton of World War II fame often said, "Every man needs a pat on the back sometimes; some need it high, some need it low."

Sensitivity

Basic to understanding is sensitivity. People will not always tell you—in fact usually not tell you—their feelings. You must in most cases read their faces, watch their body language, and interpret their actions to identify their current feelings. This is complicated by the ability of some people to mask their feelings so it is hard to tell what they are thinking. Faces—and eyes—are the best indicators of inner feelings.

There are no set rules that apply to all people for interpreting feelings. Understanding of the individual over a period of time, and being aware of changes in expression, manner, or habits give clues to changes in feelings. Obviously, then, to be aware of changes you must first have made observations from which you can detect changes. This realization brings you back to the prior principle of learning to know your people. If you look at this part of your work as a fascinating exercise in observation, it will greatly assist you in doing it.

Sensitivity to people truly means sensitivity to the change in people. All of us apparently have a sort of normal behavior which we portray most of the time. Thus, you are looking only for changes from that norm—which simplifies your task. Usually in a group of 5 to 7 people, as few as one or two will appear to be behaving somewhat differently from their normal. These are the ones to check on and see if there is really a problem at this time, or not. The better you know your workers, the easier it is to spot the changes.

What to do if you seem to spot a changed behavior. A simple technique which is difficult for anyone to object to is to ask, "Are you all right today?" Facial reaction to the question will usually tell you quickly whether the words in response are accurate or not.

Some people are always "all right" but their eyes or face or both say differently. A follow-question depends on your understanding of that person, but something like this is usually acceptable, "You seem to be bothered by something and I just wondered if there's any way that I can be of help." And MEAN it!

Self-Image

This is what a person thinks of himself. A good feeling about yourself frees you to do things because you have confidence in your ability to perform. Many people have a poor opinion of themselves and their abilities. "I'm no good at that," often means "I don't want to try" or "I'm not able to do the job perfectly, so I'm not worth anything."

Persons with poor self-images usually need encouragement and rewards when they attempt their tasks. Overconfident or inflated self-images need restraint. How these acts are related to the person involved determines their effect—and the reason you need to know your people.

There is the story of the salesman who drove a subcompact and made $400 a week (the story is from some years ago.) Then he wrecked his car and was given a full-sized car as a loaner while his subcompact was being repaired. For the six weeks it took to repair his small car he made $600 a week. After his subcompact was repaired and returned to him, he went back to making $400 a week. He believed more in himself when he drove the bigger car than he did when he drove the smaller one.

Sincerity-Honesty-Integrity

Your sincerity will affect your own ability to be sensitive to others. If you are not sincere in your actions, it will ultimately become known. Interestingly enough, other people can detect insincere actions very quickly, and be turned off by the insincere supervisor.

At the same time, sincerity is a relatively easy thing to mask to some people. Words can appear to be sincere. Even some actions. But over a period of time, your true sincerity will be accepted by your workers if your words and your actions are consistent.

Unfortunately, over the years the techniques of inquiry about worker's wives and children has been touted by some behavioral "experts" as the way to show your interest in the workers. And, of course, it can be. What you say and do *after* the inquiry, however, will determine whether your question is sincere or not. Insincere inquiries of this kind by a supervisor, destroys faith in his personal honesty. A tragic loss because most people value honesty and fairness as the major qualities they like in other people.

Honesty is more than not stealing something that belongs to others. In a supervisor, it means being truthful in your statements to your workers. One of the greatest compliments your workers can give you is: He does what he says he will do and he'll tell you the truth as he knows it. People will respect and work for a supervisor about whom they can make that statement.

Integrity is an extension of honesty and applies to all aspects of your behavior. It means that you live by your word; that you have respect for other people, and that you accept responsibility for your own actions.

Regardless of sometimes disparaging remarks by some, the vast majority of workers prefer to have a supervisor with integrity. They know where he stands, they can rely on his statements, and they will receive fair treatment. People with integrity make mistakes. When they discover them, they admit them, make what corrections are possible, make apologies where necessary, and proceed with their work. You can work for a person like that! And so can your workers.

Your workers have these same qualities of sincerity, honesty, and integrity in varying degrees—as probably you do. Treating all of your workers as if they have these qualities in their highest sense is valuable to you. For those who do, indeed, have these qualities in the highest degree, they will respect you for realizing it and respond to you accordingly.

For those where these qualities are less developed, your assumption of a high degree of sincerity, honesty, and integrity may cause them to assume these characteristics to a greater extent than they otherwise would. A big advantage for you.

Workers deficient in these characteristics will probably reveal themselves to you fairly quickly. You should discuss these weaknesses with the workers and if there is no improvement, arrange to have them leave your unit as soon as possible. You cannot build a strong organization on people you cannot trust, and folks with these flaws cannot be trusted. Your principal job is to build a productive unit of workers. Workers without sincerity, honesty, and integrity will not build a sound work force.

Because people are so different, and different at different times, you can improve your skill of understanding people by exposing yourself to as many people as possible.

Supervision is a people job. Understanding people is,

therefore, the basic ingredient of getting people to perform as you would like them to.

Like most other things, the more practice you have in your basic skill, the better your chances are of improving it. Mildred (Babe) Didriksen, Olympic gold medalist and one of the greatest women athletes of the 20th Century, was once asked, "Isn't it wonderful that God gave you all that great athletic talent?" Babe responded, "Yes, it certainly was. But those 10 hours a day that I practiced didn't hurt anything either."

Make a habit of meeting with as many different groups of people as you can, then observing them carefully to see if you can gain an understanding of each person. This can be fun, as well as educational. Many people like to meet other people but are too shy, or afraid of rejection, or for some other reason, to make the first approach. You'll get mostly good responses to a friendly approach to people. Use your name as an opener: "Hello. My name is (George Boddiger). How are you?"

Names

Some of the most important words to you in any language are your own name. It gives you identity and a feeling of appreciation when someone uses it in addressing you.

When introduced to someone, always give your first and last name, and ask for theirs if they don't give theirs in return.

Be sure you pronounce the other person's name correctly and spell it right. Little things wrong with pronunciation or spelling bother people immensely. My name has no "n" in it, but countless people spell it "B-o-d-d-i-n-g-e-r" (possibly because English has few words with an "ig" but many with an "ing".) Small thing. But important to me. You probably are the same way about your name.

A valuable supervisory tool is the proper use of names. It is something you should be very careful to handle correctly because of its direct impact on how people think about *you*.

In addressing people, use Mr., Mrs., Ms, or Miss or the professional title such as Dr., or Rev., or their first name. In no instance should you use *last* names only. There is something vaguely insulting about using only a person's last name, and something friendly about using a first name only. Unless there is a climate in your organization that dictates differently, a supervisor usually has better rapport with his workers if he uses their first name in his contacts with them. In some few cases where you are *much* younger than one of your workers, use of Mr., Mrs., etc. may be more polite at the start. Usually such people in a unit, however, prefer to be treated like everyone else and will ask you to use their first names. If they do please do so. (An 83 year old director of my company who was 30 years older than I at the time and whom I'd been calling Mister, asked one day, "Call me Clyde. I want to be one of the boys.")

Use of first names gives a friendly impression. Lack of using *any* name in talking with another person, causes a reaction that you are unfriendly. In one of the early sensitivity training courses many years ago, the consulting psychologist was giving a brief description of each person in his session, as he and other people interpreted them. To a young, very bright, and competent young man, he said, "People see you as being unfriendly." "Why?" asked the startled young man. "I say 'hello' to everyone when I meet them!" "True," replied the psychologist. "But you never say their name, such as 'Hello, John'. From this, people have inferred that you haven't taken the trouble to find out who they are and therefore you are unfriendly."

A valuable insight.

Be no respecter of persons in using names. Say "Hello,

(name)" to everyone you meet whether it is the lowest paid person in the place or the chief executive. (You may want to call the CEO Mr. , or by the appropriate title, unless the habit in your company is to use the first name for even the top organization people. To do otherwise might give the image of a smart-alec, or worse—someone who does know the "rule around here" but is trying to curry favor.)

There has been a tendency in the United States in recent years to increase the use of last names only. Many newspapers have adopted this practice, which is unfortunate. Amazingly, a recent issue of *The Washington Post* carried an editorial on a convicted criminal in which he was referred to as Mr. while in their regular news columns they usually refer to people by their last names. It is further interesting to see that this same impudence does not apply to the highest government figures as-they are still referred to as President Bush or Secretary Baker.

As a contrast, *The New York Times*, which is commonly accepted in the USA as perhaps the finest newspaper in the country, continues to use full names or proper titles in later mention of those people in news stories. *The New York Times Manual of Style and Usage*, which governs the composition of this paper says: "Mr., Mrs., Ms, and Miss are to be used in news stories not only for citizens of the English speaking countries but also for citizens of other countries who do not have royal, noble, military, religious, or other titles of the kinds that replace the foreign equivalent of *Mr., Mrs., Ms or Miss*. "In almost every instance, Mr. is to be used in second and subsequent references to an adult male who does not have a title of the kind that replaces the ordinary honorific. . . "In almost all first references to women—married or single, well known or not—given names should be used and the honorifics Mrs. and Miss should be omitted. Mrs. and Miss should be used in subsequent references for women who do not have titles of the kind that replaces the ordinary honorifics.

Thus, "Golda Meir, former Prime Minister of Israel, is taking her first real vacation in years. Mrs. Meir is spending it..."

Objectives

You probably have your own goals—in your company and in your life. Other people have theirs.

Most workers do not have well defined career goals, especially when they are just starting their work experience. But some do.

It can be considered a valuable contribution to your workers, and to your true interest in them, if you can get them to think about what their ambitions are, in concrete terms. No lawful or moral objective is bad if that is what a person really wants to achieve. It is not up to you, or anyone else except the individual, as to what his goal is. It is just important that some thought be given to it so that the person can proceed towards its attainment. Not having any goal is, of course, also a goal and may be acceptable to some people. But not for most people if they really think about it.

Humorist Dorothy Thompson once said, "If the average person would give as much thought to his future career, as he does to his next two weeks vacation, the results would be miraculous." This comment may not apply to everyone but it does to many.

As a supervisor it helps to know each worker's personal objectives because it will help you understand what that person does, at least some of the time. A worker taking accounting in night school might want to strive for a professional accounting career. Or, he may simply have met a pretty girl who is taking that accounting course and by enrolling in it he gets to see her twice a week without being too obvious. Understanding his true goals will help you to interpret his actions.

People do not automatically replace their own goals with those of your unit (at least not at the start of their employment.) Like it or not, most of us are selfish and look to our own interests first, and other people's later, if at all. Your task is to learn your workers' goals and then try to show them how their own goals can be achieved by doing a good production job in your unit. This is not as hard as it may appear: "I want to be a doctor," can be shown to be consistent with your operation by commenting, "....and that takes money. By doing a good job on your assignments here, you can earn more money and be ready to finance your medical education sooner."

Once you know your worker's objectives, you can help him map out a course to reach it—and you'll help him along that path! On one occasion, I saved a key employee from leaving by putting in writing his objective and the actions that he needed to take to reach it , along with what I would do (and the company) to help him. We both signed it and he stayed with the company for several more years as he progressed towards his goal.

Do not fret that he may eventually leave. In the interim, you've had a dedicated worker who will be a positive influence in your unit because you are helping him to realize his goals. You can't lose.

Goals vary. Not everyone wants to progress to larger responsibilities, or do different things. My first supervisory job involved being responsible, among others, for a woman in her middle forties, who had worked for the company for many years. A new function came into the unit and I asked her if she would take it on. She refused, with this explanation: "No, thank you. I don't want to learn anything new. I can do my work all day now without thinking about it, and can think about anything that I want to. This new function would require me to learn something new and would upset my whole schedule." Since her performance on her job was outstanding, I found another way to handle the new task.

Many people do not want the responsibility for new things, or for other people. Know their feelings and you'll save yourself a lot of mistakes and headaches.

You will be more successful as a supervisor if you realize that your personal goals and those of your workers are probably different. It is important, however, that the workers understand the goals of your *unit*. People work better if they understand *how* to do something and *why* they are doing it.

The goals of your unit should be clear in your own mind. If they are not, ask your supervisor to clarify them in specific terms until you are clear. Most important. If you don't know what your unit is supposed to do, how can your workers ever understand their jobs?

There has been much management literature in recent years about the Japanese management system of total consensus on objectives by everyone involved in the company. There can be no argument that the Japanese system works. *Why* it works is much more complicated.

Recently, Japanese firms have introduced their technique into their American plants. It seems to work there also—among American workers. The Americans are taught by Japanese and the implied pressure of working there probably has great impact on the system's success in this country.

Complete transference of the Japanese system to your operation is unlikely. You don't really have time to study it in all of its ramifications; and most importantly, successful imitation of another system without allowing for your specific circumstances is highly unlikely.

Rather, learn from the Japanese these basic points, because they are the mainsprings of that program:

1. All people like to be consulted about their work. It

gives them a feeling of importance and dignity.
2. Everyone can have ideas to improve operations.[3] Ask for them. See that they are tried and evaluated. Adopt those that are good and *give credit* to the suggester.

It is possible that Western workers cannot function as well in an atmosphere of total consensus as the Japanese. Individual initiative and resourcefulness have been emphasized in Western countries probably more than in Japan.

In thinking of the Japanese success on quality production, remember that the Chinese in Taiwan have also been phenomenally successful in developing productive workers under a more individualistic system with emphasis on the individual rather than the group. Perhaps it is well to stress here a supervisory principle that has wide application: Do not be unduly quick to adopt every new idea, principle, or system that is proposed.

Some will be excellent, but some will be worthless, with others having shadings of value between these two extremes.

Be willing to study, analyze, and experiment with anything that seems to be workable. But try it out first on a small scale before adopting it totally. There is an old saying: "Don't throw out the baby with the wash water." This means to be sure to retain what is good when you are eliminating what appears to be bad. A good principle to keep in mind to avoid making big mistakes. William B. Given, Jr., Chairman of American Brakeshoe Co., was a big believer in slogans. One of his favorites was: "Freedom to Fail."

He wanted his management to have such freedom and to be free from reprisals when what they tried did indeed, fail. Your top management may, or may not, accept Mr. Given's philosophy. Regardless, *small* failures will be accepted by most every management. Large failures may have such impact that they cannot be accepted, or rather, the judgment of the person responsible was faulty enough

---

[3]Clifford Goldsmith, President of Philip Morris, Inc., says, "An idea doesn't care who has it."

that he cannot be tolerated further in a position of responsibility.

Do not believe that this means that you should be unduly timid in making experiments on new ideas. It means trying new ideas in a small way, before making big commitments of time, people, or expense.

You should understand the difference between what would be considered significant by your top management, and what would not be so. Your authority as a first line supervisor is normally limited to areas where the results of your actions will not be significant to the total picture of the company.

You may feel that this approach inhibits your creativity. Very possibly it does. More likely, however, it shows you to have the willingness to innovate while remembering that "all or bust" may be a good gambling technique that may bring big returns. As a supervisory technique, though, it is a sure formula for ultimate disaster.

Make your mistakes small and you'll survive longer in the supervisory world.

<u>Reasons</u>

Years ago, my father said, "There are two reasons for everything: 1) The reason you give, and 2) The real reason."

This concept is a truth that applies most of the time to human relations.

"I am leaving for a job closer to home."

May really be: I don't like my supervisor.

"The pay here is too low. I've found a better job."

May mean: I don't believe I have a chance for promotion here. etc.

Finding the real reason for actions is difficult. There's a purpose in "giving a reason." The person believes the true reason will, in some way, be less pleasing to you than the reason he gives.

Are people really so deceptive?

They don't look upon it as wrong or deceptive. It's just easier for them to give a reason that will seem more acceptable to the listener than the real reason.

Probing for the real reason can be dangerous. People resent being forced to reveal something they believe will be disadvantageous to them. Anger, fear, bluster, silence, or a combination of emotions may result from your efforts to find the real reason.

Is the real reason important? Yes.

You cannot deal with problems if you don't know what they are. If you attempt to deal with the reasons people are giving you, you will be correcting problems that don't exist. The real problems will still remain.

Therefore, it is urgent to be sure you have the real reason for all actions in your unit. This is one of the most difficult tasks of the supervisor.

How to find the real reason?

1. Ask for the person's help in correcting the problem given as the reason.
2. Say, "Thank you for explaining your reason. It is helpful to me. I can do nothing about problems I don't know about."
3. Continue, "Are there any related problems that you think are also contributing to your action (decision, plan, idea, etc.)"
4. *Stop* and *wait* for a response. Do not say *anything* until the other person responds to your question—even if it takes 15 minutes before he answers. This is critical since as long as you talk, the other person doesn't have to. When you stop talking after asking a question, you put a definite pressure on him to reply. This pressure will sooner or later cause him to say something. Very possibly he'll start to hedge about

the real reason by saying something like, "Well, there's really something else" (or a similar comment).

5. To encourage further talk of the real reason, say, "Don't be concerned about telling me how you really feel. I respect your opinion and I promise not to be angry or upset with you, regardless of what you say."

   NOW. DON'T GET ANGRY WHAT EVER IS SAID!!!! You want the real reason. The surest way *not* to get it, is to show the other person that you can't accept the real reason without anger or retaliation—which is the assumed cause of his not telling you the real reason in the first place.

6. If you still don't feel you've gotten the real reason, ask just one more question, "If you were me and faced with the problem (reason) you've just revealed, what would you do?" It is flattering to be asked your opinion. Most people will respond in situations like this with further comments. Keep the person talking about the problem as long as you can. The more he talks, the more relaxed he becomes, which will lead to a reduction in the fear which made him give the first reason initially. Your attitude during this further talk will encourage him to continue, or it will stop him.

7. To encourage him to keep talking, listen hard to what is being said and what *isn't* being said. From time to time, nod your head to show you understand. Or ask a clarifying question such as, "Why do you say that?", or, "Is that all?", etc. Try to avoid questions that can be answered "yes" or "no". Phrase your questions so they will require a description or explanation. This will encourage the talker and lead to more explanations—and hopefully the real reason.

In many cases, the real reason may be simply that the worker wants to be reassured of your attitude towards him.

Merely talking with him may solve his problem.

The better listener you are, and the better at it you become the easier it will be for you to discern in the future, the real reason for things that happen. You will begin to get a feeling about what is said and what is left unsaid. The better you know your people, the better you will be able to understand what they are telling you—or not telling you—about a situation. You can then work on the real problem—the solution of which is the only way to achieve the end result of a productive unit.

Expectations

Purportedly there are two distinct extreme types of supervisors—the easy and the hard. Professor Douglas McGregor[4] has labelled them Theory X and Theory Y. Additional variations of this have appeared from other authors in recent years but Professor McGregor's is the fundamental work.

Every supervisor probably uses a combination of X and Y to some degree, with tendencies toward the extremes one way or the other.

Your objective is to develop a highly productive unit of workers which will hopefully further your own career and your own income. If that doesn't happen, you'll still have a successful production unit. There is nothing wrong with such an objective because in the process you should develop your workers to have a good self-image of themselves as competent, good people in their own eyes, who are part of a good unit. Everybody wants to be a winner—and a good productive unit is a winner in our economic system.

Should you try to be easy or hard on your workers? To lead by the carrot or the stick (reward or punishment)? Both, at one time or another, are probably the best solution for most supervisors. Which to use depends on the people and

[4]*The Human Side of Enterprise* by Douglas McGregor, McGraw-Hill

the circumstances.

Being easy or hard refers to your supervisory technique—not to the results you want to achieve. Your supervisory objective has already been fixed and doesn't change: a highly productive unit.

People generally respond to their surroundings and the expectations others have of them.

If your unit is made up of productive workers, effectively performing their duties, most persons will tend to want to keep pace with the atmosphere which surrounds them. The best general example of this is mob psychology. Persons not normally willing to undertake some aggressive action are often propelled to do so by the people around them, until they are yelling and moving with the mob.

Likewise, it has been shown in schools that a class where almost all the students get good grades will stimulate laggards to do much better than they have been doing, or might reasonably expect to do. It's been this knowledge that has helped to create the growth of classes for students with high scholastic abilities so that all of them may perform better because the students around them all perform well.

On this assumption, your good performing unit will cause new members to do their best to maintain that good performance. In somewhat high-flown language this is called "peer pressure." In everyday language, it means "Joe isn't going to be any better than me, or I'm as good as Joe and I'll show him!"

People also respond to your expectations of them. Most people do not want to disappoint others by failing to live up to those people's expectations.

An instance where I gave an assignment (to move our rather large office to a new location) to a woman associate was later revealed to me when she said, "I was petrified when you asked me to arrange the whole move of our office, but you apparently felt I could do it and I determined to live up to your hopes." Incidentally, the project was handled superbly. No one else in the organization ever realized she had never handled a job like that before.

Perhaps the secret of the above story is that I actually believed she could do the job and never indicated to her or anyone else that there was the slightest doubt but what it would be done well.

Expecting a lot from people is both a challenge and a help to them. Most people can do a lot more work than they actually do, even though they think they are fully employed. It's been said that most people use only about 40% of their abilities with the truly productive perhaps reaching 60%. So all of us have a lot more potential than we use.

People react to the expectations of others in order not to disappoint those who have confidence in them. Some years ago a fellow worker and I were given a difficult task which we were unsure about being able to complete. It involved expending a sizeable amount of money which our superior had said was approved if we needed it. During our discussion of the confidence placed in us by our boss, my associate said, "Well, let's do a good job on this because we can't let Howard down—he believes we can do it." We did a good job and I'm sure we worked harder than we otherwise would because we wanted to live up to Howard's expectations.

From time to time, I've heard many people commend a former supervisor by saying, "I liked working for him because he got me to do more than I thought I could." Self respect grows with accomplishment. All reasonable people like to have a good feeling about themselves. Doing a good job gives you a good feeling.

Another reason for expecting a lot from each worker is that none of us knows really how much we can do until we have too much to do. Results from some workers have been surprising—to themselves and their supervisors—when work assignments have been increased, often beyond anyone's belief that they could be done.

In some organizations there may be union antagonism towards improving work output per worker, although in recent years it appears as if the majority of the union's now realize that increased output per worker is the true base for compensation increases. The comments in this section are not intended to suggest that workers should be put under undue and unrealistic pressure for productivity. Merely that a person's productivity often is unknown to him and his supervisor. For the benefit of all—worker, supervisor, and company—it is desirable to increase worker productivity in all proper ways.

Motivation

Multitudes of books have been written on motivation. Countless meetings, seminars, conferences, and training sessions have been held on the subject.

There are some basic facts about motivation that you should remember:

1. Motivation is personal. Only a person himself can motivate himself.

2. As a supervisor, your task is to create an atmosphere—working condition—in which the worker responds by motivating himself to do a good job.

As a supervisor, you are a catalyst for motivation but you don't directly do it—since you can't.

Providing that encouragement (atmosphere, or whatever it is called) by which your workers decide to do a good job is your responsibility.

Inevitably, you will create the atmosphere which is consistent with your personality, and your understanding of your job.

If motivation to do what your unit needs done in order to be productive is a personal matter for each worker, you obviously must then know what each worker needs in order to motivate himself. That's what this book is attempting to give you. In three words it is:

KNOW YOUR WORKERS

You have to fit your motivation technique to each person, since all people are different, and different at different times.

Many people feel insecure—for a host of reasons. Some supervisors prey on this insecurity to get people to perform. Be careful if you use this technique—it can backfire.

Many supervisors believe that strong emphasis on rewards is more effective than harsh punishment. An old proverb is "You can catch more flies with honey than with vinegar." I believe it.

Examples of rewards that work with most people: extra privileges, bonuses, time off, variety of tasks, interesting special assignments, etc. Remember: rewards must be earned and distributed fairly based on performance, or their value is lost.

Caution

In your desire to know your people, and to get them to perform in your unit, do not try to be a psychologist or psychoanalyst. Your task is to understand what is happening and then apply usable techniques to create a smooth running organization. There is no call for you to be a reformer to try to change your workers personality.

CHAPTER 4 ──────

GOALS GET YOU THERE

James Thurber in the Preface to *Fables for Our Time* tells the story of a Sea Horse who went out to find his fortune but met an Eel, a Sponge, and was eaten by a Shark as he searched for a shortcut, ending the fable with this warning:

"The moral of this fable is that if you're not sure where you're going, you're liable to end up someplace else."

No one performs any task without a goal—whether he realizes it or not. Even lying in the sun has the goal of relaxation.

Established goals, however, lead to accomplishment. Partly, at least, because the doer does not stop what he's doing until he reaches his goal. If you set a goal of walking a mile, you continue until you reach the mile marker. Without the goal, it is likely you will stop long before that.

Production units have goals, almost without exception. But big goals must be translated into smaller ones to be manageable.

For example, production of 10,000 units per month seems high. If there are 20 working days per month, however, a goal of 500 units per day seems more nearly practical. With a work force of 5 people, a goal of 100 units per worker per day now seems as if it can be reached.

Breaking bigger goals into daily or even hourly goals gives them more meaning and makes them seem reachable.

But the goal must be established if your production unit is going to perform well.

Your workers need to understand what the goal is and why it is essential that it be reached. These explanations should be as simple and straightforward as possible. Knowing what is required and why is one of the most effective means for gaining workers' cooperation. Nearly all people truly want to do worthwhile work. If they understand what is required of them and the relationship of it to the rest of the enterprise, most people can enthusiastically perform their duties. Not having that information makes people feel unimportant or in some way inferior. With such feelings existing, it is difficult to work enthusiastically.

Do not be concerned that the what and why should be complex or sophisticated. For example, "Our goal is 500 units per day from our production unit. This is 100 from each worker. This number is needed because the department that uses the output from our unit needs 500 per day in order to maintain its operation. They are dependent on us to keep their operation running smoothly."

Many supervisors find it helpful to keep a graph relating to the goal of the unit. Some use a simple "thermometer" like the one on the next page. You've seen these used often in local United Way and other charity drives.

Keeping score is an essential part of goal setting. It's like a game and the enthusiasm for a game stems directly from score keeping. If you watch a "pick up" game in any sport, where there is no score being kept, it soon degenerates into an individual show-off contest, or a boring occasion, and the game stops—or someone begins to keep score. Add score keeping into the pick-up game and suddenly all the players become excited and enthusiastic. Keeping score in the work place will accomplish the same thing.

Thermometer Chart Month of _____			
Units	Where We Are	Where We Want to Be	Working Days
11,500			
11,000			22
10,500			21
10,000			20
9,500			19
9,000			18
8,500			17
8,000			16
7,500			15
7,000			14
6,500			13
6,000			12
5,500			11
5,000			10
4,500			9
4,000			8
3,500			7
3,000			6
2,500			5
2,000			4
1,500			3
1,000			2
500			1
0			0

Occasionally, adding an incentive like a hamburger cook-out for the worker and his spouse (or girl friend) if the goal is met, adds further interest. You can improve the interest if you agree to buy the hamburgers and buns if the goal is met. Or any variation of the idea that seems to appeal to the group—perhaps letting them decide how the reward will be handled, or even what the reward will be (within reason and your finances, of course.)

Many successful supervisors ask the workers to help set the goals for a unit. This brings worker participation into the process and makes the goal "their" goal rather than "yours". People appear to work harder to achieve goals they have helped to set.

In actual practice, most often there is a minimum goal required by the company and the goal then determined by the workers is something more than that.

All people seem to like to play games and keep score on how they do. You might as well gain the benefit of this most universal American characteristic.

CHAPTER 5 ————

MANAGE YOUR TIME

Your time is your most important resource. You've been aware of it before, but now that you have supervision over other people the value of your time hits home hard.

Wasted, or ineffectively used, time is lost forever. Because your time is limited, use it wisely on your most important tasks.

Try to do the essential tasks every day. Make a simple daily task list in their order of importance:

Date:

Today's Most Important Tasks:

1.

2.

3.

etc.

Cross out the ones as you accomplish them. Add on new ones that come up during the day in the spots their importance deserves.

Make this list either every evening before leaving for home or first thing every morning, as suits your preference. BUT MAKE IT EVERY DAY!

Origination of the idea of a numbered task list and working on it based on the most important tasks, reputedly came from an assignment, around the start of the 20th century by Charles Schwab, the great industrial steel maker, to Napolean Hill, an innovator of great resourcefulness, to come up with a plan to improve Mr. Schwab's personal effectiveness. Here's what transpired:

"Show me a way to get more things done each day," Mr. Schwab declared. "If it works, I'll pay you anything within reason."

Mr. Hill reflected, then later rose to the challenge.

He handed Mr. Schwab a piece of paper and said, "Write down the things you have to do tomorrow. Mr. Schwab did as requested.

"Now, number these items in the order of their true importance," continued Mr. Hill. Mr. Schwab did that.

Finally, Mr. Hill instructed, "The first thing tomorrow morning, start working on Number 1 and stay with it until it is completed. Next, take Number 2, and don't go any further until that is completed. Then proceed to Number 3, and so on. If you can't complete everything on the schedule, don't worry. At least you will have taken care of the most important things before getting distracted by items of lesser consequence. The secret is to do this daily—evaluate the relative importance of the things you have to get done, establish the priorities, record your plan of action and stick to it.

"Do this every working day," Mr. Hill went on. "After you have convinced yourself of the value of this system, have your men try it. Test it as long as you like. Then send a check for whatever you think the idea is worth."

In a few weeks, Mr. Schwab sent Napolean Hill a check

for $25,000.00. It is reported that Mr. Schwab later stated that this idea was the most profitable one he had ever learned in his business career.

In five years, the "$25,000 idea" was largely responsible for turning what was then a little known steel company into one of the largest steel producers in the world. It also helped make Charles Schwab a multimillionaire.

Be careful of time wasters that are fun: 1. Having coffee and chatting use large amounts of time unless watched carefully, 2. Telephone calls that last 20 minutes when the work to be done in them could have been handled in five minutes (the telephone is a great convenience and a great time waster, too.), 3. The "drop-in" visitor—who comes by and stops to talk. Usually, they are friends you like. Too much time can be lost by prolonging such pleasant occurrences, 4. Excess conversation around a real problem. Much time is wasted by spending a half hour on a 5 minute decision. Fit the time to the importance of the task. Oftentimes, the more common the problem, the longer it takes to get an agreed-upon solution because every one involved understands the problem and wants to give his opinion.

At the Board meeting of a large company it was reported that there were two items on the agenda: approval of a $26 million power plant, and the repair of the bicycle shed at the rear of the plant property. The power plan resolution took 10 minutes to discuss and pass. Repair of the bicycle shed took almost three quarters of an hour. Reason? No one really understood the complex power plant issue and accepted the recommendation of the staff, but everyone understood the repair of the bicycle shed and wanted to contribute to the discussion.

One technique for helping you to understand how your time is spent, and thereby cause you to improve your own work habits, is called a Time Ladder. This is a simple device which requires only paper, pencil or pen, and a hand-prepared form like this one shown at the end of this chapter.

Starting with your arrival at work and continuing through the entire day, by five minute intervals, record in the space beside each time exactly what you do in that time. For example, show on the form: Resolve problem with Sam on the copier, (NOT: Worked with Sam.) Indicate everything you do in the time slot allotted, such as: Called home to check on tonight's party, or Coffee, etc., Do the recording immediately as you complete each action. Do NOT wait until the end of the day or even the hour—you'll lose track of what you actually did. Do it *right now.*

Review each day's ladder at the end of the day. Prepare a weekly summary by general categories of activity:

Coaching hours
Supervisory discussions
Assigning work
Solving production problems
Telephoning (business)
Telephoning (personal)
Wasted time
etc.

Use as many different categories as you think you will find useful.

Two weeks is probably a maximum you'll have to do this because you'll be struck by the facts: You're wasting a lot of time, or perhaps more kindly, you're spending too much time working on some things than those things really deserve. You may be working on things that someone else could do. Assign them elsewhere and free your time for more important things.

Use of a Time Ladder will be one of the most important supervisory tools you have because it will show you whether you are spending your own time properly on your supervisory duties. If you aren't, the Time Ladder will show you where to find the time to spend on the things of importance to your supervisory success.

You can have your workers keep a Time Ladder, too. It will do the same job for them, unless they are on a straight production type task where they have only one type of work to do and output is easily measured. In such cases, perhaps, keeping a Time Ladder to record time required to handle interruptions such as telephone inquiries, other worker inquiries, and such, could be very helpful.

TIME LADDER		
Date	Name	
8:00 } *Morning*	9:05	
8:05 } *coffee*	9:10	
8:10	9:15	
8:15 } *Assigning*	9:20	
8:20 } *work*	9:25	
8:25	9:30	
8:30 } *Telephone*	9:35	
8:35 } *call—May (sick)*	9:40	
8:40	9:45	
8:45 }	9:50	
8:50 } *Coaching Jim on new*	9:55	
8:55 } *project*	10:00	
9:00	10:05	ETC.>

CHAPTER 6 —————

WHO SHOULD DO WHAT

Your most important daily production task will probably be work assignments, unless your processes are prescribed from some other part of the company. Even in those circumstances, you can make good recommendations for changes because you are the nearest management person to the process. Work is being done under your direct observation. No one should know more about the tasks to be performed, by whom, and in what time frame, than you.

If you are responsible for the allocation of work in your unit, and most first line supervisors are, some format of how to do it should be useful. The Work Assignment Chart is a simple way of reviewing the distribution of work and helping you to identify changes that could mean improvement in output.

The sample Work Assignment Chart at the end of this chapter is in a form which you can easily construct yourself, for your own operation.

After completing the chart, analyze the assignments given to each worker to determine if there is a more advantageous way to allot the work. Are there possibilities that some functions can be combined? or eliminated? One of the surest ways to improve output is to eliminate unnecessary steps completely.

Consider each of your workers, to determine if the tasks assigned to them are consistent with their abilities. If not, then determine what changes can be made to utilize more effectively the skills of the workers in your unit.

Assignments are not written in stone—they can be and should be changed when your review indicates the need.

Some supervisors have success with getting their workers to review the Work Assignment Chart and give their suggestions. Your workers know even more than you do about the jobs they perform and can often identify desirable changes to improve the units performance. Another advantage of letting your workers review the Work Assignment Chart is the feeling they get from it that they are important to the operation of the unit. Since they are indeed important, obvious good can come from letting them know it. The ability to decide actions to be taken is what makes a person important. Let your workers get this feeling by seeking their ideas and suggestions.

There has been much written about the Japanese management systems of Quality Circles and their consensus related worker involvement in unit problems. The opportunity for workers to be involved in work assignment is a form of participation that will generally be much appreciated by workers. An old truism: Everybody wants to be somebody; nobody wants to be a nobody.

Be prepared for differences of opinion. People do not always agree with each other on what is best, or even what may be the most desirable alternatives. During such exchanges of opinions among knowledgeable people, you will often be led to better conclusions than you may otherwise have reached. Don't be afraid to make a decision that will adopt one course of action over another, regardless of which of your workers may have made it. Your response to the question as to why you selected the option that you did can always be, "That way of doing the job just makes more sense to me, and since I have to be responsible for the output of this unit I have to make the final decision on what to do." No one can argue with your being responsible, and getting the blame if anything goes wrong.

Different types of businesses and organizations have different work distribution problems. You can adjust the basic concept of the Work Assignment Chart example to fit your needs. The principles of showing what each worker does on each task, or the tasks assigned to him, applies to all units.

Variety

Variety is indeed the spice of life. It relieves boredom and creates interest. Try to have some variety in the work day—every day. In work assignments, try to arrange tasks so there is a change of activity as often as possible to relieve the tedium of doing the same thing all the time.

Time spent on introducing variety into the work day will result in better output and more productive workers.

All jobs can be made interesting with some imagination. The story is told of the bank clerk whose job involved verifying endorsements on checks. He decided to make it interesting by observing the payees on the checks and associating them with the names of the drawers. He noticed some interesting facts which he later used to testify in a law suit identifying that the checks had been paid to known racketeers—whom he recognized on checks from a certain businessman! His bank won the case because of his alertness and initiative.

In evaluating work distribution, it is well to keep in mind the considerable value of a current trend toward assembling entire products in one location. Evidence seems to indicate that variety and pride in starting—and finishing—a product results in a form of worker satisfaction that is hard to duplicate in a flow process.

Another benefit is often the elimination of inspection steps as these can be relegated to the end of the construction of the product, since corrections will be handled by the same workers who completed the initial steps. It also brings home the lesson that doing it right in the first place will speed the whole program, thereby increasing productivity.

Adopting this philosophy only adds value to the work distribution concept as it must also be used in identifying the units to be constructed, as well as the Flow Chart Principal in the next chapter.

WORK ASSIGNMENT CHART				
Activity	May Grade 10 Hr.	Sue Grade 8 Hr.	John Grade 7 Hr.	
Mail	Verify all outgoing mail 10	Respond to special requests/ Obtain data 20	Deliver special checks 2	
Inquiries	Interview callers 5		Analyze inquiry requests/ Obtain data/ Dictate letters 18	
Payments	Maintain Acc't. Payable Jrnl. 8 Request Chks. 10	Adjust vendor records (orders/ payments/other changes) 12	Audit payment requests 20	
Records	Keep prod. records Prepare prod. reports 5	Process rec. reports 8		
Misc.	Train new employees Cross training 2			
Total	40	40	40	

UNIT _____ DATE _____

Helen Grade7 Hr.	George Grade 7 Hr.	Jane Grade 4 Hr.	Hazel Grade 4 Hr.	Total Hrs. Worked
Prepare all outgoing mail for mailing 10		Open and distribute incoming mail 20	Open and distribute incoming mail 19	81
	Analyze cash and credit inquiries 5			28
Prepare checks 30	Compute cash requirements 10 Prepare pay-ment requests 25			115
		Operate inscering & copying machines 19	Obtain acc't. records 10 Enter data in computer 10	52
		Prepare & process maint requests 1	Maintain unit supplies 1	4
40	40	40	40	280

CHAPTER 7 ──────────

GET INTO THE FLOW

A Flow Chart is a picture of how the work goes through your operation. It is another tool to use in diagnosing the work of your unit.

There are two basic types of work flow: job and process.

Job flow: where the entire task assigned to your unit is given to one person and he completes it by himself.

Process Flow: where each worker, or group, in your unit does a part of the job and then passes the work to someone else in your unit to do another part of the work. The completion of the product may be accomplished in your unit, or just some part of the whole, and the product is sent to another department for additional processing.

The difference between the two lies: In a job flow, the work is done by one person or one group doing all the steps following a set sequence. In a process flow, the work moves from person to person, following a sequence of steps from one to the other.

To make it easier to identify the various types of activities that take place in any operation, some more or less standard symbols have been used so as to make analysis easier:

O transportation (movement of something from one place to another)

Δ storage (when something remains in one place)

☐ operation (when something is being created, changed, added to, etc.—some action takes place)

⬡ review or audit (when something is being inspected, checked, audited, reviewed, etc. The primary purpose of this action is to verify that what has already been done is accurate.)

These symbols help to spot such things as too many storage stops, too frequent transportation, too many audits, etc.

Look at the Flow Chart at the end of this chapter. There are 10 storage points. All of these result in time in which nothing is being done. Some of the questions that might be asked are: Can some of these be eliminated? Can some be combined to reduce the number (could #2 and #4 be done at the same time? etc. There is only one inspection. Is that enough? Should it be done earlier to avoid working too long on material with errors? etc.

Flow charts can be used for process systems or job systems. The example above is for a process. The same procedure is used for a job system. There are the same operational, storage, and inspection steps, and may well be steps involving "transportation" where the worker goes somewhere to obtain materials or take an action. Evaluating step sequences is equally productive in increasing output in both job and process situations.

This analytical procedure can be applied to computer operations in the same manner, since computed activities also involve the same basic activities.

Your purpose in making a flow chart (job or process) is to be sure that every step taken is needed. Be diligent in applying your mind to each step. Don't accept excuses such as, "We've always done it that way," or "We've already tried the way you suggest and it didn't work."

The most important questions to ask are:

1. Can this step be eliminated? If it can, that is the best simplification possible.
2. Can this step be combined with another?
3. Can this step be simplified to make it easier to accomplish?
4. Can the sequence of steps be changed to improve output?

One technique for obtaining ideas is called brainstorming. (See Appendix 9.) It works if you follow the rules. Try it.

Think about your new ideas for a day or two before renumbering them. New thoughts require time to be digested before they begin to be understood. "You can't make pickles by pouring vinegar over cucumbers. You have to let them soak a while," is an old proverb.

Don't try to investigate all ideas at once. Start with the most important and follow it through to a decision to adopt or to reject it at this time. Then proceed to number 2 and repeat the process with the 10 most likely suggestions. After taking each of those 10 to a conclusion, hold the list for your next meeting to see if any of the remainder are still worthwhile.

The value of this gradual approach is that neither you nor your workers are overwhelmed by the size of the task.

Forcing the investigation of 50 ideas is a staggering prospect. It will intimidate you and keep you from starting. If, however, you actively check out the 10 best, you know you've attacked the potentially most valuable ideas. Your results from these should provide worthwhile improvement in your unit's operation. Your next meeting will be that much more productive because of the results from the previous one. Success in an endeavor encourages further effort. Studying and considering projects without any tangible results breeds apathy and disenchantment with a process.

If you have at least one successful idea from every meeting, you and your associates will retain your enthusiasm—and further good results will be assured.

Initiating Changes

Most people prefer to continue their present ways. Making changes requires effort and a break from the familiar.

One idea for getting a change tried is to ask the worker to try an experiment. Most people can't refuse an experiment because it implies a *temporary* condition. It is also difficult to refuse without admitting a closed mind.

Once the experiment is underway, the value of the change will become apparent (or not) and adjustment can be made.

An experiment must run long enough to make the new method become familiar. Doing something new always takes longer than doing something familiar. (Ask someone to write his name leaving out ever other letter. It will take much longer than writing the name in its usual way, but it is obviously only *half* the work.)

Another value of the experiment approach is the involvement of the worker in the development process. You want his help. No better way to get it than to let him be a part of the process—to conduct the experiment. Then you can seek his opinion of the proposed change and his ideas for improvement. And WOW—it becomes <u>his</u> idea. For which you give him full credit.

Remember two Human Relations Principles:

1. You can do a lot of good if you don't care who gets the credit.
2. The more credit you give away, the more people will give to you.

Transportation	Storage	Operation	Audit	Step No.	FLOW CHART
					Activity: *Processing checks* Date:
O	▲	□	O	1	Incoming mail received
O	△	■	O	2	Open mail
O	▲	□	O	3	In stacks
O	△	■	O	4	Sort mail by type
O	▲	□	O	5	In sorted stacks
●	△	□	O	6	Take check mail to cashier
O	▲	□	O	7	On cashier's desk
O	△	■	O	8	Read mail
O	△	■	O	9	Remove checks
O	▲	□	O	10	Letters in "hold" basket
O	△	■	O	11	Enter check amounts and identification in computer
O	△	■	O	12	Update computer accounts for payment.
O	▲	□	O	13	Checks in hold basket
O	△	■	O	14	List checks on bank deposit tickets in duplicate
O	▲	□	O	15	Checks and deposit slips in hold basket
O	△	■	O	16	Run tape on checks and balance
O	▲	□	O	17	Tape, checks, and deposit slips in hold basket
●	△	□	O	18	Take checks, tape, and original deposit slips to bank
O	▲	□	O	19	Place duplicate deposit slip in hold basket
O	△	■	O	20	Mark letters as handled
O	▲	□	O	21	Letters in hold basket
●	△	□	O	22	Take letters to file cabinet
O	△	■	O	23	File letters in alphabetical file folder by name.
O	△	□	●	24	Verify total checks in computer with deposit slips
●	△	□	O	25	Take duplicate deposit slip to file cabinet
O	△	■	O	26	File duplicate deposit slips
4	10	11	1	26	

CHAPTER 8 ───────────

Undoubtedly your company will keep records of output from your unit. The kind kept for the company may not be as helpful to you as a supervisor, as your own. In any event, you need to know what your workers are actually producing in order to treat each of them fairly in accordance with what they produce.

Simple observation of your workers often is misleading because of the varying ways that workers perform. Some form of written record of output is essential.

Some years ago in an organization where I was at the time, the need for production records was discussed with a new supervisor who had been promoted from a clerical position in that same unit. "I've done this work and I know who produces and who does not. Besides, I can see all of them all the time all day long so I'll know if they are producing or not," he responded. "Will you try an experiment?" he was asked. "0. K., but it's a waste of time," he asserted.

During the period the study was being conducted it was established that 11 units would be a good day's work since the handling of each unit took a long time.

Two weeks later, we summarized the results. The supervisor was astonished. His best worker, as he had judged him, was producing 2 units a day! His actual best worker was someone he thought was average—but he was producing 20 units a day. A difference of 10 times between the poorest and the best. More surprising was the realization that personal observation had been so misleading. His actual highest producer had been given only normal salary increases while the poorer worker had been given above average increases. Very unfair but without actual records you can't be sure of your impressions.

As a significant result of this experiment, the supervisor and I discussed why he was misled by his two workers. We finally decided it was because the poor producer was always working diligently. Never obviously wasting any time. Came on time. Took only permitted lunch and break times and never left early. All the apparent earmarks of a good worker. The reason, of course, was that he needed all that time to make his contribution, minimal as it was.

The other worker was gregarious. Did, in fact, waste time occasionally and never seemed to be working very hard. He didn't need to, naturally, to make a good production record so he didn't try as hard as he really could.

Personal observation cannot replace accurate documented facts in evaluating any situation.

Keep your own records, so you do indeed know who in your unit are your good and poor producers.

Simple records are all that is required. List the names of your workers down the left side of the page and the days across the top. Enter each workers production by day and total the days production. At the end of a week, or other convenient period, total the production of each person. Results for a period are more significant than those for one day because you are looking for consistent application rather than an occasional outstanding day.

Use of the production record to discuss performance with each worker can be most helpful because it focuses attention on the proper base for discussion—productivity!

On the following pages are simple production record forms which you can use as models to adapt something similar for your own use.

Regular Meetings

You need some relatively formal system for meeting with your workers to discuss their work problems and to get their ideas and suggestions on how to make the unit more effective.

One approach is to start with a 15 minute meeting once a week for the purpose of raising questions (by you and your workers), suggesting changes in operations, or discussing anything of general importance to you and your workers.

When to hold such a meeting? Your unit work load will be fundamental in selecting a time for your regular meeting. Pick a period when the unit work is slower than normal or just before a peak workload. Frequently, Monday morning is suggested and that is fine if there is a lull at that time. Friday is sometimes selected because you can also use the meeting to help plan next week's schedules. On the other hand, Friday is often especially busy as everyone tries to get as much work out as possible before the weekend.

Sometimes, midweek works well for many supervisors because the meeting time can be fitted into the schedule and still meet the unit's deadlines for the week.

When your staff is well trained with experienced

workers, frequency of the meetings can be reduced to every two weeks or monthly. This you will have to gauge yourself.

IMPORTANT: Regardless of frequency, the meeting should be specifically scheduled for time (starting and ending) and place for the specific day selected. This should be announced to all workers and the schedule kept religiously. If there isn't enough discussion to last the allotted time, close out the meeting early and disperse. The ending time for the meeting should be understood as the maximum limit, so that each worker can arrange his schedule to make maximum utilization of his time.

Constant Productivity Growth

Economists have said repeatedly that growth in wages, individual living standards, and the well-being of the country comes ONLY from gains in productivity. It appears as if we are finally believing it as the USA economy has been registering huge increases in productivity, making USA products competitive in cost in world markets and increasing exports for more than nine straight years.

If productivity is the "secret" to the success of a country, it must also be the "secret" for a business organization. Since your unit is a major factor in the generation of the product of your company, or it wouldn't be around, you should obviously be deeply interested in the productivity of your unit.

You already have most of the tools to increase productivity in your personal history records, organization chart, work distribution chart, output chart, and score keeping mechanism. It only remains to put them together to show your productivity gains.

Before you start that process, you may want to speak to your supervisor to see what other supervisors are doing to keep track of productivity per unit, or the company may have a standard format for producing this information.

If there is nothing to copy, perhaps you can devise your own productivity record so that you will know what your unit's results are.

The elements of productivity are the mixture of capital, labor, and management. Very likely your management will not release such data to you, or do not have it at the unit level. No concern. Your principal goal is to establish the labor value of each unit completed by your group. This can be provided effectively for your unit by maintaining a record of the total hours worked each day by your workers and comparing it with units produced. (The units produced may be the total product, if you are organized that way, or the units you consider finished and provided to the next process.)

This information can be accumulated daily in a chart—or in the computer—in the following manner:

Production Record
Units

Worker	3/3	3/4	3/5	3/6	3/7	Wk Total	Remarks
May	70	71	72	73	73	359	
Sue	81	81	84	80	86	412	Good week
John	62	62	63	65	68	320	Progressing
Helen	40	35	30	~~TERMINATED~~		105	Couldn't adapt
George	78	78	78	79	79	392	Good
Jane	65	65	65	65	65	325	Discuss w/ J.
Hazel	68	68	69	68	67	340	Discuss w/ H.
Alice				20	25	45	Started 3/6
Total	464	460	461	450	463	2298	

Production Report
Unit Summary
Year ____

Week Ending	Weekly Total	Remarks
1/5	2,010	
1/12	2,016	
1/19	2,025	
1/26	2,100	
2/2	2,101	Proper Trend
2/9	2,050	1 New worker
2/16	2,160	
2/23	2,210	
3/2	2,211	
3/9	2,298	
3/16	2,400	Change in Distribution Method

Productivity Worksheet

Date	Number of Units Produced	Number of Hours Worked	Productivity Units Hours
3/3	464	56	8.29
3/4	460	56	8.21
3/5	461	56	8.23
3/6	450	56	8.04
3/7	463	56	8.27

Your objective is to keep the number of units completed as high as possible with the total number of work hours as low as possible—hopefully with the number of units increasing and the number of total work hours per unit decreasing.

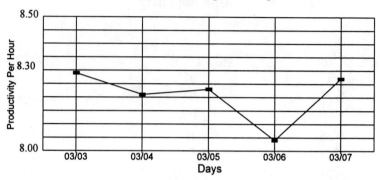

CHAPTER 9 ———

PICKING THE RIGHT WORKERS

You may not have the option of final selection of the workers in your unit. If you do not, then this section can be skipped. If you do, read on.

You've realized from what has been written before that people come in many varieties. How can you determine which ones to hire for your unit?

Experience is perhaps the greatest teacher in selecting people. You don't have that when you start, so here are some points to look for when interviewing a potential worker for your unit:

1. Look briefly at education and personal data shown on the application form. These are less important in most beginning workers than other considerations. School grades should probably not be at the very bottom level, however. Remember that good school grades reflect an ability for sustained effort which is valuable in a

work situation.
2. What has he done before?
    2.1 If just out of school, did he work during vacations? in a summer job, or after school jobs?
    —If he did, was his record good?
    —Did he like his work? Why, or why not? Listen.
    2.2 If no work experience, what did he do other than simply attend school?
    —Is there some evidence that he tried to do something extra?—play sports, do volunteer work, participate in other school activities? Did he hold positions of leadership in these activities?
    —If so, these would be evidence of a willingness to do something more than just get by. A desirable trait.
3. "Why do you want to work here?" The reasons should be logical and honest. "To earn money" may be an honest answer that is more desirable than some high minded purpose that is given because the applicant thinks you want to hear that.
4. "Will you do what you are told by your supervisor?"
    4.1 Most applicants will quickly say "Yes" because they want the job. If the answer should be "No"—be sure that's what is meant and then dismiss this candidate. You cannot operate with someone who won't do what he's told.
    4.2 Later, if the candidate is hired and a question of doing what he's told comes up, it is most helpful to be able to refer to

the initial interview in which you said that willingness to follow instructions is essential. This eliminates the objection, "I was never told that."

5. "What are your goals in life?" To young workers this may be the first time anyone has ever asked this, and they will have no reasonable answer. No problem. What you are looking for, though, is the unusual person who may have established goals for himself. If he has, you probably have an above average candidate. Ask for more information about his objectives, listen to his reasons. If you listen hard enough you'll find out if this candidate will fit into your unit and be productive. Much will be revealed about himself if he talks about his goals. Goals are what drives people to accomplishments. Having something to work for, makes better workers. Remember that goal-oriented people are achievers—a quality you want in your workers.

6. "What have you started that you've completed? What haven't you completed?" You want to find out the candidate's ability to be a doer and a finisher. Most early jobs in an operation require continuity of effort, even if the tasks are repetitive and possibly boring. People who complete tasks they undertake usually make good beginning workers—or at any level for that matter. Honesty is the objective in the second question. If the candidate's answer is "None", ask more questions because that answer is unusual. Nearly everyone has some things he has started and not finished. There should not be many, however, and the reasons should appear appropriate.

Long time industrial psychologist Donald A. Laird in

his boot *The Technique of Getting Things Done* suggests the following question in interviewing prospective workers:

"What were you working for in your last job?"

"Ninety-nine out of a hundred applicants will give their last salary as an answer. They often hopefully name a higher figure, if they thing they can get away with a little stretching.

"But the hundredth says he was working for some specific goal—he wanted to learn the business, to buy a house, to get married, to lay by for independence by the time he was fifty.

"Keep your eye on that hundredth man."

You are looking for these four characteristics that are present in all good workers and absent in very few:

1. Character

    Unless the basic qualities of good character are present—honesty, loyalty, trustworthiness—you cannot build on the person.

2 Reliability

    Will he do what he says he will do? and what he is told? These are basic to a good performer. You must be able to rely on what your workers say they will do. If you can't, then your job is impossible.

3. Reasonable intelligence for the job.

    Usually this means only a level that most people have. The vast majority of beginning jobs can be learned on-the-job. If the worker is able to understand the job instructions, then he generally has sufficient intelligence to do it.

4. Willingness to work.

    4.1 You cannot achieve your unit's goals unless your workers actually work. Persistent effort on the part of your workers to get their tasks done will offset most other deficiencies. Without that effort, your unit will not perform its proper function.

4.2 Tied in with willingness to work is that elusive but critical factor called desire. It is usually reflected in willingness to do what is necessary to do a good job. Desire is the most difficult factor to identify. It comes closest to being revealed in the answer to "your goals" question. In it's best form, desire means that quality in a person that causes him to do everything necessary to reach his goals. Obviously, to have this quality it is necessary to have the goal. Hence the relationship to the goal question in the interview. No one knows where desire comes from exactly. Nor why some people have it strongly, and others do not. In my opinion, desire comes from having a goal to accomplish which is so important to the person that he will strive to achieve it regardless of the obstacles involved.

One of my associates had a 15 year old daughter, Lisa, who decided when she was 13 that she wanted to be a doctor. She became a candy-striper in a local hospital at age 13, working after school, on weekends, and during the summer. In school, when asked to write a theme, she chose medical subjects, then visited doctors to get first hand information on her subject to add to her research in the library. Her grades were straight "A" because, she says, "You have to have good grades to get into medical school." This is no bookworm, however. She's a cheer leader for the school team, she's captain of her school's girls field hockey team, and is beginning to notice that boys exist. None of these activities, however, has changed her goal of becoming a doctor. Do you believe Lisa will be a doctor? I do. How did she develop this desire? No one can be sure but my suspicion is that the goal inspired her to create the desire.

You should be interested in looking again at those sample qualities of a good worker in this chapter. Notice that many things which are talked about as qualities of a good worker are not included here—superior intellect, good home, outstanding grades in school, etc. It is true, and comforting to most of us who may not have outstanding academic or intellectual credentials, that those things are not needed to be a good worker. What IS required are characteristics that *everyone* has—*if he wants to have them.* Keep these characteristics topmost in your mind as you interview people. If the candidate convinces you he has these four qualities he will probably be a good worker for you. It is highly unlikely that he will be a good worker if he doesn't have them.

Reduce chances of bad selection by choosing only those you believe have the four basic characteristics:

1. Character
2. Reliability
3. Reasonable intelligence
4. Willingness to work

CHAPTER 10 ———

"How Am I Doing?"

Everyone wants to know if he is performing satisfactorily and if he isn't, what is wrong with his work.

Telling people where they stand is probably the greatest weakness at all management levels. You can shine as a supervisor more easily by keeping your workers aware of their status with you, and their fellow workers, than by any other single action.

Most companies recognize this element and require at least a yearly "performance appraisal." Unfortunately, this procedure is usually lazily enforced and there is often more lip service than solid results.

One of the inherent difficulties in these performance appraisal programs is the once-a-year time table. Events come and go during the year. The good is often forgotten and the bad is often remembered. Time and subsequent events blur reality.

You can best meet the needs of your workers for

knowing their status by planning a frequent (every month or so—but fairly regularly) meeting with each worker for a few minutes (not over 15 minutes at a time) to review how he's performing his job. This can be a good opportunity to review the worker's personal file that you keep, and discuss any entries you have there. You should note in the file any comments the worker has about his job and his performance, for later consideration.

Specific strengths or weaknesses in the worker's performance should be discussed, and corrective action agreed on if needed. It is essential that these comments be in specifics—not generalized. "You have made four serious errors in the past two weeks. One was . . . . etc." NOT: "You aren't doing very well lately."

Dwell on a worker's strengths and suggest ways even they can be improved. Again, be specific. If someone is especially accurate in his work, see if he can reach "zero-errors" status. Of course, improving his weaknesses are important. Again, be specific. If two significant errors were made last week, talk about them with him. Why does he think they happened? What has he done to keep from making the same mistake again? What does he think he should do NOW to avoid future repetition? Try to get specific answers and later note them in his Personal Record file (Chapter 2) for future reference. Conclude each meeting with your worker with some specific word of approval and encouragement. These types of meetings are not for severe discussions but merely for keeping in touch, and for current status.

Next time you talk together, review your Personal Record file before and start the discussion by referring to the suggested actions from the last meeting, to see if proposed suggestions were really followed through.

On some occasion through the year, you should probably complete a simple assessment form (or your company one) to picture the worker's standing at that time. Staggering these reviews throughout the year will keep the task manageable, as well as reduce the gossip on "your rating" that occurs when all are done at one time.

A review form can be as simple as this one suggested on the next page—or more elaborate if you prefer. (Many companies have a standard form that is required, but use of your own is also worthwhile for your own records.)

Hard as it may be, and subject to all the hazards of misunderstanding, anger, frustration, etc., on balance, it is probably best to share your Record Review with the worker involved. This is best done by asking him to review your comments (prepared either by you in advance, or together during the discussion) and to write his own view of your observations.

This procedure seems consistent with the fundamental purpose of a review—to let the worker know how and where he stands. If you keep your comments secret from him, or do not allow him to make his own observations, how can good results be expected?

Some management students believe it is also very important for individuals to know how their bosses' boss feels about them. In first line units, this may be difficult because the next supervisor above you often does not have a chance to get acquainted with your workers and what they do. If it is possible, however, from time to time in your periodic reviews, try to let your workers know the feelings your boss has about them—if not individually, then as a unit. Hopefully, the opinion will be favorable but, if not, your workers should know about it and the reasons for that opinion. This evaluation comes best from you, rather than as gossip from workers or supervisors outside your unit.

RECORD REVIEW	
Name (worker)	Date
Supervisor	
Principal Strengths	
Principal Weaknesses	
Suggested actions to improve strengths	
Suggested actions to help correct weaknesses	
Overall Rating 1————————————————10	
Worker's Comments	

CHAPTER 11———

TIME FOR A RAISE?

People do not work for bread alone—but most people <u>do</u> work for their pay to greater or lesser extent.

Regardless, pay is important and rewarding workers in accordance with their contribution to the output of your unit is a major part of your responsibilities.

In thinking about a system to administer salaries, it is fundamental to establish that plans do not usually provide for automatic increases (except possibly in the first months of employment when workers are basically in a beginning training status and automatic raises are given to signify that the training has been learned—and those who don't reach that level are terminated.) Salary administration systems are established for the purposes of <u>considering</u> workers for increase in pay rather than guaranteeing an increase on the basis of some plan.

It is a maxim that it is not totally important to get a raise at every time permitted in a plan, but it is vital to be

<u>considered</u> for an increase at the chosen times in the plan.

Presumably this principle relates to the worker feeling that he will be treated fairly if his performance is properly reviewed on the same schedule as other workers. This concept of fair treatment to all is central to a good supervisor.

<u>When To Consider Raises</u>

There are four principal times, often debated, about when to give raises:
1. Once a year (or more frequently) on the worker's anniversary of employment.
2. All at the same time for all workers (often in December or January, of each year.) Normally only once a year for those with the company for a year or more.
3. Any time you feel like it.
4. When a worker asks.

Once a Year (or more frequently) on Anniversary of Employment

Relating ordinary increases to the anniversary date of employment has many advantages: it spreads out the work load of considering raises over the entire year; it gives a logical time to talk to the worker about his performance and to give a reward for it at that time if a raise has been earned; the interval can be set at most any time you desire. Some supervisors give a modest increase several times during the first year (3 months, 6 months, 9 months) and yearly thereafter, or any variation of this arrangement.

One caution in using this system for wage increases is to relate the compensation of all the workers in your unit so as to be sure that your superior performers are properly paid, and that all workers are paid in proportion to the level at which they perform. Since you are considering only one or two workers at a time you are making your recommendations, it is easy to overlook the comparison to the others in your unit.

It is wise in using this plan to make a check of all salaries after you've decided on your recommendations in order to be sure the relationship among all your workers is kept the way their performance justifies.

All at One Time

This system has the advantage of giving you an excellent opportunity to look at all your workers at the same time and to grant increases in accordance with the relative performance of each worker.

The serious disadvantage of this system is the tremendous temptation of all workers to compare their increases with the ones received by the other workers. If you've done a perfect job, the fairness of your decisions will probably be accepted—except that each person usually sees himself as equal to at lease some of the others, and inevitably there will be unhappiness with their increases on the part of some.

It is useless to caution people not to discuss their pay with other members of the unit. People just seem inevitably to get the information somehow with occasional disturbing results.

When You Feel Like It

This is the system often used by the more autocratic-type supervisor who oftentimes wants to show who's boss.

This plan is also a favorite of supervisors who believe the spontaneous pay increase can be used as an immediate reward for especially good work, or upon completion of an assignment, or similar occurrence.

The disadvantage of this plan is that it can lead to favoritism, can badly skew the pay levels of the group, and often overlooks the steady, but unspectacular performer.

This plan is not recommended for supervisors because of the disorganized appearance it gives to an operation and real dangers it creates through inequitable treatment.

Occasional on-the-spot increases can sometimes be used in very special circumstances but such action must then be related to the rest of the group and balance restored in your regular raise program to offset any bulge created by the special increase to one person.

When a Worker Asks

This system has only the advantage of quelling one worker's demands at a given time.

Its disadvantages are: the worker is assuming the initiative in salary administration, rather than you doing so as the supervisor; temptation to treat more generously with the more aggressive of your workers rather than the most competent; repetition of requests ("It worked before, I'll try it again"); the effect on other workers who see the aggressor getting raises so they will start using the same tactics; the haphazard nature of the requests and the results, may greatly distort the relationship among your workers based on aggression or salesmanship rather than merit.

It's generally conceded that this system—or lack of a system—is not a desirable plan to use on a regular basis.

There are times when a worker's request for a raise can be used by you to review your salary administration plan to see if it is giving the kind of fair results you really want. There may have been a breakdown in your following your plan, or the inquiring worker may have been overlooked or unfairly treated. If so, do not change your basic program but arrange to correct any unfairness within the framework of the system. Tell the inquiring worker what you will do and when—and then be sure you do what you say at the proper time.

Use of Personal Record

When you are considering your pay adjustments, your Personal Record file will be indispensable. If you have been diligent in keeping your record, you'll have entries to jog your memory of good and bad situations with each worker during the period under review. Having a written reference on what's happened will give you confidence that you can treat each person fairly, to his advantage, and to the satisfaction of your other workers.

Evaluation Process

Your objective in considering each worker is to evaluate his performance in relation to what you both agree are his responsibilities for quality and quantity of work. It is also realistic that each worker's performance will be compared with the other workers. A common and simple evaluation system is to rank each worker in comparison to the others with the best performer at the top of the list and the others following in order of performance.

If the pay program is administered fairly and there is any increase money available at all, some workers should get more than others and some, possibly, may get nothing. If you are given an increase budget, either in dollars or per cent of payroll, you will want to apportion the amount on the basis of performance, rewarding your best with the highest increase and down to the least effective with the lowest raise.

Resist the temptation to give everyone the same dollar or per cent increase. This is not being fair unless everyone is performing at the same level of competence—which may sometimes occur. If so, the same per cent is fair, if the base pay is equitably established.

Be firm in rewarding good workers, and in telling those who don't qualify for increases why they weren't getting them—and what they need to do during the next interval to qualify for a pay raise.

Review the preceding chapter on "How Am I Doing?" to refresh your memory on what to cover in talking with workers about their performance, and see how it relates to awarding pay raises.

Accurately assessing each worker's contribution to your unit's production and seeing that he is paid fairly in relation to his contribution—and in relation to the contribution of the other workers—is a critical function of your job as supervisor. Doing this well, and explaining your actions to each worker about his own situation, will go a long way to establishing your competence as a fair leader with favorable relations and work responses from your workers.

In some companies, there are rules that establish grades, or levels, for each position. In most cases, however, there is a range of pay within each level and the supervisor should be in the best position to determine where in the range each worker fits.

You will normally be involved in the process of establishing, or reviewing, pay grades and possibly the ranges, for the workers in your unit. This will involve evaluating the importance of each position and relating it to the general descriptions of the pay grades. Participation in this process will further clarify for you the relationship of the production importance of each position to the others and give you a basis for determining pay levels as well as work assignments based on your evaluation of each individual.

Salary administration and evaluation systems are an

extensive and sometimes complex problem. For more advanced information on the subject, check Appendix 8 for references.

CHAPTER 12 ──────

COACHING MAKES A TEAM

Coaching is the technique of imparting knowledge to others through instruction, demonstration, and correction—repeated until the task can be performed by the student to the standards established. Coaching in the requirements of the tasks assigned to each worker is a most important element in your new responsibilities as a supervisor.

In recent years, it has become popular to say that the new breed of young workers are more demanding in their attitudes. They want to know not only what they are to do, but why. They also are less concerned about how to do their tasks because they believe their education makes them competent to decide how best to achieve the desired results. Use of the coaching system brings good results with these workers.

Whether these characteristics of the so-called new breed are really much different from what has always been the case is problematical. More advanced education by more people may have caused them to feel better equipped to decide the "how." It may not. Recall how hard an unfamiliar task was to you the first time you tried it? Did you immediately know the best way? Probably not.

The old saw of reinventing the wheel is at least partially appropriate here. Formal education is difficult to apply directly to the usual daily work tasks of a beginning job. Much better to accept that this is the way this job is currently being done.

"After you've mastered it in its present form, no doubt you'll be able to think of new ways to make the job easier and to increase effectiveness. When that time comes, please be sure to talk to me about your ideas." Reasonable people should accept this approach. So-called intelligent people who cannot accept learning how the job is currently done, are probably less intelligent than they believe.

Remember the story of the husband who said to his wife, "How many really intelligent men do you think there are in this town?" Her response was, "I don't know, dear, but there is one less than you think there is."

Introduction to the Job

Perhaps the most important coaching time is the introduction to the job the first day. Your new worker is eager to learn and wants to do a good job. You will have his attention and he will accept what you tell him.

Because everything is new and there is so much to learn, it will be hard to remember everything—so concentrate on the most important elements, and give him the Task List for his job for later reference.

After the introduction the first day, don't forget the new worker. Frequent checks on, "How are you doing? Any questions?" will show your interest in his progress and relieve some of the apprehension that exists on a new job.

It is during the introduction that you will have your best change to emphasize the importance of the job and its relationship to other work in the unit.

This is also the time to emphasize the rules of the unit. The new worker will accept them now and, if necessary at a later time, can be reminded that the rules were explained to him on his very first day and he accepted them at that time.

It also eliminates any "surprises" for the worker when he knows what the rules are in advance.

One of the values of coaching is the confidence it instills in the worker who has received it. Feeling secure in knowing what to do results in improved performance by everyone. Coaching also permits workers to learn new skills, to relieve monotony, to use imagination, and to create hope for future advancement.

More often than not, the success of a supervisor lies in his ability to teach his workers so they perform their tasks quickly, accurately, and on time, the FIRST TIME. Productivity comes from doing things right the first time they are done. This fact seems obvious, once you're thought about it.

It has often been said that it's a shame that people do not have time to do their tasks right the first time, because they always seem to have time to do them over. Eliminating the "do overs" frees important time to add to the total output.

Cross Training

Teaching another job in your unit to a worker, in addition to the one he performs regularly, is called cross-training. Ideally, it would be perfect if every worker in a unit knew every other job in the unit. It is possible to achieve this goal and to benefit greatly from it. Because of turnover, and other factors, it often isn't possible to have everyone cross trained on all other jobs at all times. Best to keep trying, though, and cross train as many as you have time to do. It is a continuous job which pays big dividends over the long run. Unfortunately, because cross training takes time and therefore may reduce immediate output, it is often delayed until some future date when pressures for output won't be so great. That time often never comes and the cross training isn't accomplished.

Keep a log of the workers who have been cross trained and in what jobs so you can refer to it quickly when occasion demands, such as sickness, vacations, peak loads, absences, etc. A sample of an easy cross training log is given below:

Cross Training Log									
Name	Postion	Position and Date Trained							
		1	2	3	4	5	6	7	
May	1	✕	3/28		4/5				
Sue	2		✕						
John	3	2/19		✕		4/16			
Helen	4	Terminated		3/6	✕				
George	5	5/2				✕			
Jane	6						✕		
Hazel	7							✕	
Alice	4						Started 3/6		

Coaching Tools

Many aids to helping new workers have been devised over the years. Here are some: job descriptions, duty cards, procedure manuals, critical task lists, job breakdown analysis, training manuals, teacher-pupil conference, role-playing, programmed learning, and others. All have value in some circumstances, and all have the same objective.

Hopefully, you are in an organization with good training help. There usually is some form of assistance in larger organizations. Often, in smaller firms the task is left solely to the supervisor. We'll assume that is your situation. Then what to do?

After much searching, some variation of the desk manual, or work station task list, seems to offer the most practical teaching tool for the realistic training job facing every first line supervisor. This can be very simple (or complex if you want to make it that way.) It is basically a list of tasks to be performed at a particular work station. (See sample at the end of this chapter.)

There is no need to make the Task List any more formal than filling in the form shown. In many ways, simply asking the present worker to complete this list in his own words is adequate. When samples of output can be attached, they are always helpful.

One of the major pitfalls of this simple coaching tool is the demand by someone (a staff assistant or similar) that these lists be standardized with a set format for uniformity. This is not essential for the basic purpose, although possibly desirable in a large company. All that is really required is clarity and completeness. Everything else is frills. As a supervisor, you'll learn that frills can be nice but they frequently add cost, time, and effort over that actually needed to achieve cost-effective results.

One successful user of a Task List has each worker fill out his own Task List and the supervisor reviews each one with the worker involved to determine if everything is covered and understandable. This whole procedure of writing the lists and the supervisory review is a matter of a few hours at most in the majority of situations. It is not a gigantic job when handled as described above. It can become a huge operation if it gets over-engineered by involving too many people outside your unit.

One technique is to set aside 2 hours at a specific time when every worker in your unit will prepare his Task List. Since all will be working at the same project at the same time, there will be fewer outside interruptions and more attention directed to the Task List preparation because everyone is doing it at once.

To make sure that corrections are made, you, as the supervisor, must review the Task List for each work station once a month without fail. Unless you add this regular monthly review, the entire project will collapse. If you are dedicated to getting these lists prepared and kept current, you and your associates will benefit mightily. Workers will be confident they are doing what they are supposed to; you will be confident that each worker knows what to do and when, or has a ready, accurate reference to check to determine what and when.

Training of new workers is immensely aided by the Task List. Nothing is left to chance. The work to be done at each station is completely and accurately set forth. New workers have a ready reference to check their understanding of what they are supposed to do. Temporary absences can be better handled because anyone reasonably familiar with the unit will be able to fill in since there is an accurate and complete guide to follow.

Cross training is greatly simplified by the Task List. As one person expressed it, "It gives you a track to run on."

You know where you are going and where you are supposed to get.

As a supervisory tool for effective management of the work your unit is expected to perform, there is no better technique than the Task List. And no simpler one to install and maintain.

Like most effective tools, the Task List is simple and easy to understand. Keep it that way, and check to be sure it is completed and up to date at all times. It will do a superior job for you.

Work Improvement

Review of all Task Lists at one time with your entire unit can be a most effective work improvement device also.

Set aside a period of one hour once a quarter, where all Task Lists are reviewed by your entire group with the idea of developing improved ways of getting your work out. Use the brainstorming technique described in Appendix 9 to get the most out of your workers' suggestions and get the ideas flowing.

After all the emphasis on coaching how things are to be done, it is wise to recall that the objective is to achieve the desired result. It is not really important as to how the result is achieved so long as the method is not illegal or immoral, and includes all the required data.

Policy Manual

A useful tool for management and for coaching is a Policy Manual. This is a loose leaf binder with copies of letters, memoranda, or comments relating to principles agreed upon in connection with questions raised, or actions taken. By keeping a book with these decisions recorded in it, you can avoid having to request an answer on a similar problem that may arise in the future, as well as provide for consistency of action on related matters.

Establishing a subject divider in the book makes it possible to put the material in categories for easy future reference. An index in the front by subject, is also essential.

Since this is a reference for you and your unit, the exact method of setting up the book and keeping it current is a personal matter which you can decide for yourself with your workers.

Your workers should know where this book is kept and that they have free access to it at all times. Knowing where to find guiding principles of operation when needed will relieve you of the burden of answering repeated questions on the same subject, and assure consistency of performance whether you are present at the time the question arises or not. A valuable device.

Task List

Name Mae		Position Lead Clerk A/P	
Date Prepared 6/1		Location Home Office	

Daily Tasks

No. of Items	Time To Do	Description	Equipment Needed
40	2 Hr.	Verify Outgoing Mail	Adding Mach.
3	1 Hr.	Interviewing Callers	Telephone
100	34 Hr.	Maintain A/P Records Requesting checks	Typewriter, Add. Mach, Computer
1	1 Hr.	Production Records	Adding Mach.

Weekly Tasks

4	1 Hr.	Summarize Prod. Rec.	Adding Mach.
4	1 Hr.	Total Journal A/P Forward Results	Computer

Monthly Tasks

4	1 Hr.	Summarize Prod. Rec.	Adding Mach.
4	2 Hr.	Total Journal A/P Bal. & Forward Results	Computer

Quarterly Tasks

3	1 Hr.	Summarize Prod. Rec.	Adding Mach.
3	2 Hr.	Total Journal A/P Bal. & Forward Results	Computer

Yearly Tasks

4	1 Hr.	Summarize Prod. Rec.	Computer
16	4 Hr.	Yrly Totals Journal A/P Complete Yearly Totals	Computer

CHAPTER 13 ——————

"YOU'RE LATE AGAIN!"

Most workers, unless their job is in a production line type of activity, see little sense in the supervisor's being upset by a few minutes of tardiness.

Some of your best workers will frequently be the most chronic tardy offenders. Your immediate reaction is not to offend those who have high output. Especially since the low producers are often the most careful about being on time.

What to do?

Finding the real reason for the tardiness is obviously the first step. This is usually difficult. Tardiness excuses are limitless and the brighter the worker the more ingenious the excuses.

On chronic "tardy-ites", some supervisors keep a list of the excuses used so that it can be reviewed to see a pattern. One supervisor who had a young man on his staff found that the young man had been late on six different occasions over a period of time because of attending his grandmother's funeral. Six grandmothers is above the normal supply!

This episode is reminiscent of the young lady who reported a lost bathing suit on her income tax form as a tax deduction (back in the days when such a small loss was deductive.) It worked so well that she lost one every year until the tax authorities decided such carelessness was probably not a matter of true casualty loss. Upon questioning her, she admitted, "It worked without any questions before, so I just decided to continue using it."

One common reason for tardiness among better workers is the attention they receive by always being late, and the resultant sense of power they feel by being tardy and "getting away with it" because of their good work record.

What to do?

Find the real reason! But it's tough to do. Start with the reasons given:

Reason: "I overslept."
Solutions:
> 1) Buy an alarm clock.
> 2) Buy a new alarm clock.
> 3) Ask a friend to call on the telephone.
> 4) I'll call you on the phone when I get up.

Reason: "Heavy traffic"
Solutions:
> 1) Start earlier if this happens regularly
> 2) Change routes
> 3) Leave earlier and have breakfast near the work place.
> 4) Determine days of heavy traffic and start earlier or change routes on those days.

Reason: "I can get all my work out by the end of the day, even if I'm late coming in."

Solutions:
> 1) Change or increase the work load.
> 2) Suggest change of job to utilize abilities, if the reason is true.
> 3) Productivity increases from full day's work can result in a pay increase.
> 4) Effect of tardiness on people who can't get their work out in a full day.

Reason: "I work late to make up for my tardiness."
Solution:
> 1) Other people who come on time do not know you work overtime, and resent the appearance that you are given special privileges not available to them.
> 2) Your good work is appreciated, but your tardiness makes it difficult for me to recommend you for promotion or salary increase. Your value to the organization and to yourself would increase if you eliminate this negative factor on your record.

If the problem is the sense of power and privilege the tardy worker feels by his action, talk to him about the rewards he can achieve by eliminating this unfavorable habit and gain real power through promotion in position or money. Consider some visible recognition of outstanding work (including promptness) which can be earned by the worker to get the recognition that he seems to want. A chance for you to show your ingenuity in coming up with an incentive to break the tardiness habit.

Since tardiness excuses are limitless because of the imagination often used by the offenders, you, as the supervisor, have an opportunity to use your imagination in suggesting solutions to the reasons given while you search for the real reason.

Once the real reason is known (for example, frustration at not getting your job), a remedial program can be developed.

Doctors say that treatment is easy once a proper diagnosis is made. Your diagnosis—finding the real reason for the tardiness—is therefore your primary duty. Once you know what is *really* causing the tardiness, you can create a solution which will remedy the problem.

No one seems to know precisely <u>why</u> people are reluctant to state their real reasons for their actions. But it is a fact that they do. Perhaps as much as any single feature of supervision, searching for the true reason for any action is paramount. Keep it ever in mind.

CHAPTER 14 ————————

NOT HERE = ZERO

People who don't show up for work can not be productive—an obvious truth but one which absentees sometimes appear to forget. "If you aren't here, you're worth zero."

Absence from work is not a serious crime if the worker simply can't be there—but it is a burden on the other members of the production team. Work must get out whether a full staff is present or not, and that is one of the supervisor's main problems.

Absenteeism often leads to overstaffing which seems a simple remedy to a supervisor. If only six people are really needed in the unit, add a seventh and when one is not present, the work can be properly handled by the six that are really needed.

There are at least two things wrong with this approach:
1. Costs are inflated by the amount of the unneeded worker. High costs work against the success of the

company. If every unit followed the same plan, company costs would skyrocket.

2. C. Northcote Parkinson[5] some years ago coined Parkinson's Law, which says: "Work expands so as to fill the time available for its completion." Shortly after hiring the seventh worker (in our example above) everyone in the unit will have adapted his expectations of his full day's work to be 1/7 of the total production, from his previously accepted 1/6 of the total output. Efforts from then on to get 1/6 of the total output from six people will be met with resistance because each worker has mentally adapted to his 1/7 work load and feels that going to 1/6 is too hard, demanding too much, unfair, etc.

Adding another worker to the staff is not the answer to absenteeism.

Most management people believe the principle to follow is: "Staff for the regular work load; handle peak loads by overtime, or temporary part time help."

There are a number of advantages to this principle:

1. It does not inflate the payroll permanently.
2. Each worker retains and accepts his normal work load.
3. When workers are required to work overtime to compensate for the absence of one of them—both those present and the one or ones absent are aware of the strain that absenteeism puts on the workers who are present. Sincere absences can be accepted under these circumstances, but excessive or improper absences will ultimately cause pressure from the dedicated workers on the chronic absentees. Either the chronic absentees will be persuaded to get to work, or the other workers will pressure you to hire replacements who can be depended upon: "We are tired of working overtime all the time just to cover for someone who is never here." Thus you get help

---

[5]*Parkinson's Law* by C. Northcote Parkinson, Raffles Professor of History, University of Malaya (Houghton Mifflin Co.—Boston)

from your workers to correct the problem or hire new people.

What To Do with Chronic Absentees

It's basically the same problem you've faced in other situations: Find out the cause of the absenteeism.

Everyone misses work legitimately once in a while. None of your workers is concerned about this and neither should you be.

People who continuously are absent are another matter and are probably:

1. Too sick to try to hold a regular job. (They should be encouraged to find a part-time job somewhere else.)
2. Uninterested in their job. (This should be discussed with them. Particularly that continued absence must result in termination. They must develop a good attendance pattern or they will be replaced.) Try to find out what does interest them and see if there are elements of the job that can be shown to coincide with their interests.
3. Creatures of bad habits. (Wanting long weekends so they are absent on Friday or Monday, or both. (Continuance of such a practice has to lead to termination. Some people contend that they simply have to get more rest, can't bring themselves to come in on Monday, etc. They must be informed of the seriousness of absenteeism and given a reasonable time—a month at most—to revise their thinking, or be terminated.) (All jobs can be interesting if you make an effort to make them interesting. See if you can create an interesting aspect to the job involved and remind the worker of that factor, and of the job's importance.)
4. There probably are many reasons that even I have

never heard but they very likely will belong in one of these broad categories. The approach to these reasons is the same: "You are being unfair to your fellow workers who are burdened by your absence. Neither they not I will tolerate it further. Unless you are here regularly in the future, you will have terminated yourself from this position."

The interdependence of each worker with the others as far as the performance of the unit is concerned is frequently not appreciated by each worker—especially new ones. It is essential to explain this, from time to time, emphasizing the seriousness of being absent, and the inevitable release that must follow. "I am not going to fire you. You are terminating yourself by your actions."

Some supervisors contend that no worker should be terminated, but he should be educated to perform properly. No one truly disagrees with such an approach. Good supervisors do show workers what they have done that causes their bad performance and what they must do to correct it. Such explanations can only be continued so long as there is improvement in results. Keep in mind that your unit cannot produce according to plan without worker performance at least equal to plan. Anyone who can not carry his share of the work load on a continuing basis must be eliminated in order for you to achieve your unit's objectives—the criteria by which you will be judged.

In many cases, termination is a help to a worker. It often gives him a chance to get a job more suited to his abilities, to go into business for himself, to get more education, or merely to cause him to reassess himself and what he wants to do with his life. Most of us who have been terminated at one time or another (and I have) have profited by the experience although it is doubtful if anyone truly enjoyed it.

Perhaps its belaboring a critical point, but handling

absenteeism requires an understanding of your people as do most other actions by a supervisor. This is where the difficulty comes in supervision. Consult your Personal Record (Chapter 2) on an offender. There may be clues there. At least enter the absences and see if there is a pattern. It is not one absence that is a problem—it is a developing trend. In the presence of such a trend, questioning of the worker is required to try to find a cause or a possible remedy.

Caution: While endeavoring to solve the problem of the chronic absentee, be sure not to agree to an action which will put an added burden on your faithful workers. Temptation to try to help the absentee can backfire on you if your faithful workers believe that you have not considered their position in your solution. You must be concerned with the faithful workers and consider their reaction to any solution you propose.

Your goal at all times is to be fair to all people involved. If your solution seems to do that, most likely all parties will accept it—and appreciate your handling.

Absenteeism is closely related to tardiness in many instances. It's just for a longer period. Somewhere in both actions there probably is a lack of appreciation for, or interest in, the job to be done. Discerning a pattern, through your records, can be most helpful to a solution.

CHAPTER 15 ——

WHEN DISCIPLINE IS NECESSARY

Much has been said about the need for discipline in running an organization. It is needed. Perhaps it's been overdone, however.

There are ways to achieve willing cooperation without the appearance of stern discipline. There are more ways than one to reach an objective.

The iron fist is one type of discipline. In civilian organizations it often does not work. Good workers resent being figuratively or literally beaten. Poor workers will accept such treatment because of their fear of not getting another job. You want good workers in terms of their productivity on their jobs. You want the best out of them.

But you can't treat everyone the same. General George S. Patton, that great World War II commander who developed the Third Army into a fearsome effective fighting force, once said, "Every man needs a pat on the back sometimes. Some need it high. Some need it low." A truism.

Your task is to find out which type of pat goes with which person.

Stern measures with one person can destroy him. The same action with another will result in immediate correction of the condition and no resentment. You must know your people and how they feel about things to decide which measures to use.

In one supervisory instance, I called in the worker and said, "Joe, sit down because I'm going to hit you with a club. It's the only way you'll understand what I have to say." I then went over the offending situation firmly with him in precise detail, explaining the mistakes made and what should have been done by him. Then I said, "Do you clearly understand what I have just told you?" He replied, "I sure do now, Boss. Thanks and I'll do it right from now on." And he did.

Proper measure for the right person at the right time.

In another instance in the same organization, I disagreed with an associate in a staff meeting, indicating that I thought another course of action was in order. Later, a friend of that worker came to me and said, "You've totally destroyed Gene by your remark. He tries diligently to do what you want and felt you were absolutely harsh on him in the meeting." In no way had I intended severe criticism but that's how it was taken.

Wrong method for that person at that time.

What should have been done? I should have said nothing in the meeting, then later had the worker come to my office and explained why I thought his course of action was not as good as the one I selected.

Which brings up a powerful principle: Workers are <u>NOT</u> to be criticized or reprimanded in front of other people! A good rule to remember is: *Compliment in public and criticize in private.*

More often than not, discipline is less formal than new

supervisors commonly expect. The purpose of discipline is to obtain willing cooperation with the required patterns needed to achieve the necessary output. To get the job done.

The words discipline, criticism, punishment, etc. cause negative responses from most people. In nearly all cases, the necessary actions can be taken without raising the hackles caused by shouting or the use of profanity. No one has the "right" to be unpleasant to anyone. Coaching is a polite word with favorable connotations that often will achieve what is needed. Think of terms that your people will respond favorably to, so as to get their willing cooperation.

Ask for help from your workers when discipline seems to be a problem. They often know what is workable and what is not.

It is important to ask for suggestions and assistance from your work associates. With this caution: tell them not to be upset if every idea they have is not accepted. Ideas from different sources can be conflicting and only one can be tried at a time.

It is important to every worker to have his ideas considered, even though they are not adopted.

An explanation of why an idea is not adopted is essential. It it's a valid reason, as it should be, most people will see it, and accept it, and be happy about it.

A further benefit of such an explanation is that it helps to clarify your own thinking and reasoning. If you can't explain something so someone else can understand it, the chances are you should review your explanation. It may be wrong rather than the idea.

Corrections

A major part of your activities will be making corrections and adjustments for such things as incorrect work, refusal by a worker to do as he has been asked, personal friction between workers, or between you and one or more workers, etc. What to do?

Many such situations occur because of misunderstandings or misinterpretation of instructions. The first step is to talk to the worker involved, separately and privately, about the situation "What is the matter?"

To correct any situation, you must first establish what is happening, or has happened.

The next step is to be sure everyone involved agrees on what is happening, or has happened.

Next: What does the worker involved thing should be done?

Why?

Next: Does the worker's suggestion seem appropriate for the situation involved? Why or why not?

—If so, adopt his solution and close the case.

—If not, and your solution seems better, explain your reasons, give your decision, and close the case.

—If not, and you are uncertain of the proper action, set a specific time later to meet with the worker again; then think of a better solution or seek help from your supervisor. Be sure to keep your specific appointment with the worker; give your decision, and explain the reasons for your action.

In the entire process, try to be as objective as possible in collecting the facts on what is happening, or has happened. Review them as carefully and as objectively as possible. *Do not get angry.* You want to be fair but firm in your fact gathering and review, as well as in your final decision.

Seek all the objective help you can find but make your own decision. If you have doubts about it, ask your supervisor to review the facts and your decision with you. If he approves your position, proceed—it is your decision. If your supervisor has doubts, he will seek help from others and get back to you with alternatives for you to consider.

Do <u>NOT</u> ask your supervisor what you should do. Propose your own solution and ask for his opinion of it.

Misunderstandings

Raymond H. Belknap, late President of the United States Life Insurance Company and a long time life insurance executive, insisted that you should never let a misunderstanding continue. Go directly to the person involved and discuss privately with him the misunderstanding—as soon as you know it exists. Get it settled as soon as possible. The longer a misunderstanding continues, the more confused the reason for the disagreement becomes. Very quickly it will deteriorate into a simple dislike for the other person and the real cause of the misunderstanding will be lost.

This course of action is not easy—but it works—to your great benefit.

One of my associates commented about one of our managers and the difficulties he had with our branch managers. "The problem with John is that the first two phone calls between him and the branch manager are about the claim. The next three are about each other!" Bad procedure.

Physical Aggression

This is more common today than at any time in the past. Do not be a hero. Immediately go to your supervisor and report the situation in detail and request immediate action from him.

CHAPTER 16 ——————

"You're Fired!"

No job is harder for most supervisors than to terminate a worker.

Usually, there are mitigating circumstances. No one does everything wrong. A worker is usually terminated or transferred because of a series of errors or lack of productive effort. Even then, there are occasions to which the worker can point where he made no mistakes, and where he put forth extra effort. It's the gray area of performance (neither good nor bad) which creates the real problem in termination. For example, there is no question about termination for the man who rapes a secretary in the hall. But short of that, it appears as if there is always something to be said for the worker.

What to do?

Record in a separate file, over a period of time those instances which together justify termination. Your Personal Record, started when you took over the unit or when a new employee enters it, becomes invaluable here. Both favorable and unfavorable events are recorded. When the unfavorable events start to outweigh the favorable ones, a warning is in order. If unfavorable actions continue, discharge is not only called for but essential for the proper operation of the unit.

Your written record can be made a part of the worker's file for further reference and support of your action.

In these days of government and personal concern about discrimination and fair treatment for all, your written entries over a period of time can not be disputed. Some supervisors even go to the trouble and difficulty of having the worker, on serious mistakes, sign that the facts are recorded accurately. This is often delicate because it leads to arguments over details and recriminations from both sides. But it is better at this time than later before an arbitrator, or a government hearing officer, or in a court of law. Indeed, such discussion often clarifies a situation by bringing out all the facts, to your benefit, and the workers.

How To Handle the Actual Firing

There's a great temptation on everyone's part to put the tough tasks on to someone else. "Let the Human Resources Department fire him," "Send him to my boss and let him fire him," etc.,

No good.

You are the supervisor and unless your organization has other rules on who can fire ineffective workers, you should do the task because:

—You should not try to avoid the difficult tasks in your job. If you do, you'll never be able to handle a bigger job.

—Your bosses will appreciate your willingness to handle tough tasks on your own without calling on them to do the dirty work.

—You will gain self-confidence by handling smoothly

a difficult task. Next time you'll handle it even better.

—You will probably learn a great deal from the experience. Every difficult action can be a learning situation for you.

—Your image in the eyes of the other workers will be enhanced by their knowledge that you can terminate a worker. Caution: the other workers must believe that the termination was justified. If they view your action as unsubstantiated by the facts, is capricious, unfair to the person involved, or unwise in any way—your image in their eyes will diminish. Is that important? Probably so. Willing cooperation is usually based on respect for the supervisor. It is not necessary, or even important, that they like you, but they must believe that you are fair in your actions. Good people will not long tolerate inept, unfair, or erratic supervisory behavior. They will leave, or search for some way to correct the situation. Possibly demanding your removal as a supervisor.

—In well run organizations, higher manager levels willingly listen to worker's complains about supervisors and often take action. One of the startling realizations to many people joining a higher management group is the concern that the group has for workers at all levels. It is generally not true that higher management is callous towards workers and their needs. In well run companies, just the opposite exists. Higher management recognizes that good first line supervision is a keystone of success. They do everything they can to see that top-quality first line supervision exists. That means paying attention to the first line supervisors' reports and to the workers' views as they arise.

In giving the worker the reason for his termination, be as specific as you can. It will help him, and require you to be sure of your facts before you start. Be prepared for his objections. It is emotionally devastating to anyone to be fired. The natural reaction in most instances is to argue that such action is not justified. If your facts are correct, repetition of them must be accepted by the worked. At that point, it is often good to say:

"We've discussed the specific errors or situations which have prompted this action. It is my judgment, therefore, that the total of these events is such that you are not the person to hold this job in this unit." (The worker may argue with the facts as you have related them but he can never disagree with your judgment of the importance of these facts in operating your unit. You have the undeniable right to evaluate the importance of the facts and reach your own conclusion. He may say that your conclusion is not correct as he sees it, but since it is your judgment he cannot dispute that. This precise way of stating the termination reason is essential. (Use it and see for yourself that it solves the problem of dispute over the facts and their significance.)

Continue:

"My judgment of your position in this unit does not mean that you can't be successful in some other position or in some other line of work. You have abilities which you should investigate so as to achieve the goals you would like to reach. May I urge you to think about what you would really like to do and then talk with your counselors, parents, or others whom you respect, to help you search out the type of work in which you can be successful. I'm sure you'll be much happier if you do.) (George Cleary, the late great President of United of Omaha, said years ago, "You can take everything away from a man but hope." Always leave everyone with a feeling of self-worth and hope for the future.) This position on your part is a completely accurate and sincere one for there is a place for everyone's talents. Since that is true, saying so at this time can be invaluable to the other person. It costs you nothing, but it gives him that priceless ingredient—hope. (If at all possible, too, you want to have the terminated employee accept the action without a deep feeling of unfairness and antagonism towards the organization. Remember that he is also a potential customer, as are his friends and relatives. Bad words and bad feelings can impact the future sales of the products of your organization. If negative impact on the sales of the products of your firm can be avoided it will ultimately be of help to everyone in the company.)

All good supervisors occasionally must terminate a worker. It should be done as quickly as events determine that termination is the only practical action. Efforts to arrange transfers to other parts of the company where an appropriate position may be available is highly desirable if such a move can be done.

Handling of a transfer is usually much easier because you are not creating a private financial crisis for the worker. Transfer can, however, be an emotional blow to the person involved. Many of the same doubts that arise in termination come up in transfer. Follow the same concept that, after the specifics of what prompts the action are disclosed, say that it is your judgment that the worker would be happier and more effective in the other department. Unless you actually intend to permit an option to remain in your unit, do not imply that such a course is an alternative.

Do not approach involuntary transfer or termination unless you intend to complete the action. If you don't intend to follow it through to completion, don't start. Give a warning instead.

Chapter 17

<u>Your</u> Boss, Your Peers, and You

It is important to your performance as a supervisor to understand that you must get along with other supervisors, and with your supervisor, as well as your own workers, in order effectively to do your job.

This sounds like an additional complication to an already complex job—and you're right. But it is essential.

You are not alone in making your company and your unit function effectively. Unless you can get along with your peers—the other supervisors—you won't make it.

More supervisory careers have probably been ruined by inability of a supervisor to work cooperatively with his peers, than for any other reason.

A common reaction to this truth is, "Why should I have to 'kow-tow' to other supervisors? It's the effectiveness of my unit that is going to make or break me." Correct. But your unit's effectiveness is controlled to some extent by the cooperation you receive from other units.

Another unfortunate truth, which you should know, is that the success of your efforts can be reduced by what other units, and particularly what their supervisors do. Such things can be deliberate and obvious, but usually are not. Some people are not that honest in these kinds of situations. Oftentimes you do not realize the actions, or inactions, that are impairing the effectiveness of your unit.

It's best not to dwell on how others can hinder your progress but rather to concentrate on what is expected of you and your unit.

Be friendly and pleasant to your peers. No one ever has too many friends. Cooperate in every way possible up to the point where you believe an action will materially be detrimental to your unit or to you personally. At that time, be firm about your position but pleasant.

Disagree without being disagreeable is a worthwhile attitude to cultivate. It gets the result you want without the side effects of raising anger or hostility in others—both of which are undesirable for you.

One way to avoid being disagreeable is to refrain from "positive" statements such as, "You are wrong!" etc. Consider saying, "It appears to me that you are wrong." This little adjustment in wording can make a difference in the mind of the hearer. The last statement cannot be challenged, because only you can say what "appears" to you.

Benjamin Franklin in his *Autobiography* (see Appendix 8 for a list of further helpful readings) describes how he found this technique most valuable:

"...I made it a rule to forbear all direct contradictions to the statements of others, and all positive assertions of my own. I even forbad myself... the use of every word or expression. . . that imported a fix'd opinion, such as certainly, undoubtedly, etc. and I adopted instead of them, <u>I conceive</u>, <u>I apprehend</u>, or <u>I imagine</u> a thing to be so or so, or <u>it appears to me at present</u>. When another asserted something that I thought an error, I denied myself the pleasure of contradicting him abruptly, and of showing immediately some absurdity in his proposition; and in answering I began by observing that in certain cases or circumstances his opinion would be right, but in the present case there <u>appeared or seemed</u> to me some difference, etc. I soon found the advantage of this change in manners. The conversations I engag'd in went on more pleasantly. The modest way in which I proposed my opinions procur'd them a readier reception and contradictions; I had less mortification when I was found to be in the wrong, and I more easily prevaill'd with others to give up their mistakes and join with me when I happened to be in the right . . . . And to this habit. . . I think it primarily owing, that I had so much weight with my fellow citizens when I proposed new institutions, or alternatives in the old."

These same attitudes will work with your supervisor as well.

Special characteristics of your relationship with your supervisor should be:

—Honesty

—Truthfulness

—Your own feelings—not what you think your supervisor wants to hear—expressed in a pleasant way.

—Concentration on <u>your</u> work and <u>your</u> problems.

—Stand on your own two feet. Think through problems carefully, reach the best possible solution—then act—keeping in mind the three types of authority every supervisor has:

1. Authority to act and forget about it.

2. Authority to act and notify your supervisor.

3. Authority to realize you do not have the right to take action, and notify your supervisor of the situation.

It is essential that you give your supervisor the benefit of your thinking and opinion but after your supervisor makes the decision, from then on your action is to support that decision.

Above all, do <u>not</u> go back to your unit and say, "We have to do this thing this way, because the boss said so, but I don't agree with it." This is a sure way to get in trouble with your boss. By trying to show the superiority of your views, you actually brand yourself as too timid to take an action in your own name, and disloyal to your boss by implying he is not competent.

Few people like to be called incompetent—even if they know they are. Truly incompetent ones will be discovered a whole lot quicker than they think they will, and without your help.

You create doubts in your supervisor's mind about your trustworthiness when you indicate to others that you publicly question your supervisor's decisions.

When you are really perplexed and uncertain about how to proceed, ask your supervisor for help. Not having the knowledge to solve every conceivable problem is no reflection on you—you are not expected to know everything. Your supervisor probably will appreciate your honesty, and your desire not to make a mistake which may be harmful to you, to him, and possibly to your company as well. Just as you must be responsible for your workers' actions, so he must be responsible for yours. Give him a chance to keep you from making a mistake—to his advantage and yours.

If you have honest questions about the decision, then go to your supervisor in private and express your views. If you are right, most supervisors will realize it and make necessary corrections. If you are wrong, your supervisor will probably explain why and if he's correct in his views, you will have learned something—a great advantage to you.

Most of all, by going in private to your supervisor you will avoid any embarrassment to him or to you. Most people do not object to being asked to explain an action or opinion more fully.

A good way to start a conversation with your supervisor in situations like this is to say, "I may have missed something, or don't have ample facts, about your decision on _____. Will you mind explaining it more fully to me?" At some point during the ensuing explanation, you can express your feelings or opinions in relation to the points that are brought up. Avoid saying this: "Your decision on _____ doesn't make any sense! I believe we really should do_____." Antagonism breeds antagonism. You will not learn anything from a vigorous repetition of what has been said before—which is likely all you will get from this kind of approach.

Your desire is to do the best job you can for your unit— and therefore yourself. Obtaining the confidence of your supervisor in your interest in your work, in your desire to learn, and your wish to be cooperative in making everything run smoothly, will work to the advantage of you and your unit.

Remember a truth from the sales field: A "soft" sell with careful reasoning will triumph over the "hard" sell every time.

Like the skills you are using to run your unit, knowing your supervisor as a person is essential. This does not mean psychological examination, but obtaining the information which will be helpful in understanding how to deal with him.

Simple things:

—Does he have a family? Is he now married? Divorced?

—How much schooling has he had and how does

he feel about education?

—What are his interests? At work? At leisure?

—Has he special attitudes about which you should be aware? (No one's perfect in his viewpoints—has he religious prejudices, racial views, etc.) Knowing such things permits you to avoid upsetting your supervisor. It is not necessary to agree with your supervisor's personal views to work effectively together. Just don't raise sore points in the work situation. Accept that there are different ways of looking at all problems.

In the event of a total disagreement with your supervisor on a *work decision*, the proper approach is:

1. Discuss it thoroughly with him in private. If you still honestly believe the action is wrong, and the issue is an absolutely vital one, then

2. Request your supervisor to go with you to his supervisor so that each of you can present your views personally together for his decision.

Obviously, this last procedure is a drastic action and you must be prepared for some antagonism from your supervisor. Therefore, this is a last resort because you may be upheld in your view which will put your supervisor in a bad light with his boss—and he won't like it or, he may be supported in his view and be resentful of your forcing him into a confrontation in front of his boss.

In either case, your boss is not going to like this experience—therefore, it's suggested only when every other approach fails and the matter is of utmost importance to you.

Still, some situations require this approach, such as:

1. Dishonesty by your supervisor, or

2. Immoral actions by your supervisor or someone over whom you have no control but whose actions are impairing the work of your unit or you personally.

3. Illegal actions by your supervisor, or orders from him to you or your unit to do something illegal.

To sum up: always act on a positive note with your supervisor. There are many people with whom he deals who are negative—against this and against that. Don't be one of them. Search for a way to help **solve** the problem, not bewail its existence or abandon it as "impossible." The only insoluble problems are ones for which we haven't yet thought of a solution—but there is one, and it can be found if it is looked for diligently enough.

Selling Your Ideas

It is often essential to try to influence your supervisor to adopt a course of action that you believe to be valuable and appropriate:

First: Identify the problem, preferably in writing.
Next: Get your facts in as much detail as possible. Make sure they are right.
Next: Analyze your facts to see what they tell you.
Next: Construct a solution to the problem (the best you can devise consistent with the costs.)
Next: Develop as many reasons why your solution is the best one possible.
Next: Suggest at least one alternate solution with supportive reasons.
Make your presentation in this order.

Regular Meeting Times

It is just as important for you to have a regularly scheduled meeting time with your supervisor as it is to have a regularly scheduled meeting time with your workers. (Perhaps once a week to start, and after a while less frequently.)

A regularly scheduled meeting gives you a chance to accumulate items that are not urgent and take them up all at once. Keeps you from running to your supervisor every time a question or situation comes up. It gives you time to think of your questions, to see patterns that may develop in them, to see repetition, etc.

Keep a written record of decisions made in these meetings and enter general policy decisions in your Policy Manual—keeps you from asking for decisions in the future on a subject on which you've already received an answer.

Chapter 18 ─────────

LET'S HAVE A MEETING

<u>Practical Techniques</u>

As a supervisor you will eventually be called on to run a meeting. In fact, a short weekly meeting of all of your workers (as pointed out in Chapter 8) is a sound management tool. Follow these suggestions for all meetings.

Some basic principles are:

1. Write down the purpose of the meeting in advance, and what decision, action, or objective is to be reached.

   —If you can't do this, don't hold the meeting—it will be a waste of time.

   —Imparting information is a legitimate purpose if that is all you want to accomplish.

2. Always have an agenda.

   —It need not be given to everyone present but you, as the leader, at least, should have one.

3. Based on the time estimated to cover the agenda, set a starting time <u>and an ending time</u>.
    —Need for a starting time is obvious. And start on time. Not to do so is discourteous to those who are present, as well as a time waster.
    —Too often, no ending time is set and discussion drags on unproductively and interminably. It's sort of a corollary to Parkinson's Law: Meeting time expands until no one has anything left to say.
    —A set ending time—with the total length kept as short as possible to get a good result—is essential because:
    —Attendants can depend on being out of the meeting at a specific time and can schedule the rest of their day efficiently.
    —Rambling comments straying from the subject, and pure "bulling," are reduced—there's not enough time to allow it.
    —Permits you as the leader to start on time because of the obvious need to end on time, and the entire period is needed.
    —Estimate the amount of time needed for proper handling of the agenda—then reduce that amount by at least 25%. An apparently short meeting period keeps the discussion on track and conserves everyone's time.
4. Assign the task of keeping the minutes to the youngest (in service) member of the group since it usually assures their careful completion. You, as the chairman, should appoint the person to prepare the minutes at the time the meeting starts.
    —Basic features of the minutes should be:
    —Name of group that is meeting
    —Date and time meeting was held, beginning and ending times.

—Names of those present.

—At least, a record of all actions taken.

—May also include major points raised on which no action was taken, or needed.

—Any assignments given, to whom, and <u>expected date of completion</u>.

—Name and signature of person preparing the minutes. —A copy of the minutes should be given to each participant within two days after the meeting. Very important. Emphasizes the significance of the meeting. Notifies everyone of what is to be done, by whom, and when.

5. During the course of the discussions be sure everyone has a chance to contribute. Ask questions of those who have not spoken.

—Cut off, pleasantly, those who delight in talking more than their contributions are worth. Reference to the time limit of the meeting can be used to soften the impact of cutting off the excessive talker.

—Questions from the leader (you) is one way of keeping the meeting on track and bringing out different views.

—Be noncommittal on your own ideas. If you are the supervisor of the group, your workers will often try to find out in a meeting what you want, and then agree. That is not helpful to you—nor is it fair to the worker who really has an idea but doesn't express it because it may differ from yours.

—Dr. Harry W. Dingman, a most effective conference leader, always called first on the newest of his unit for his opinion. Dr. Dingman's reasoning was that it showed the newest member that he was a part of the team, that his opinion was important, that he should be prepared for the meeting because his opinion would be evaluated by all present, and that opinion would not be influenced by the more experienced (and usually older) members of the group.

—Consistently getting the shyest member to talk early in the meeting will cause him to overcome his reluctance to talk. Experts have proven that once a person speaks in a meeting, he is less reluctant to speak again.

—Fear of speaking in a group may result from many factors: unprepared, fear of ridicule, uncertainty about reaction of others, basic insecurity, unwillingness to risk offense or disapproval of a person in a supervisory position, or so on and so on. . . . All of these fears recede when the person talks and discovers nothing serious actually happens.

6. Concluding the meeting. When the purpose of the meeting is reached—stop. Even if the ending time previously set has not been reached. Continuing after reaching the objective of the meeting is time wasted. It may also cause the members of the meeting to assume something more is needed and search for something further.

—Summarize the findings of the meeting and the conclusions reached on the meeting's objective.

—Record the result of the meeting in sufficient formality to indicate the importance of its being held. Minutes are essential but may be shortened to show only major points considered and any decisions reached.

It may appear that the technique of meetings as described above is cumbersome. It is to some degree. But meetings should not be called lightly because of the great hazard of time wasting. By agreeing with yourself to follow this meeting guide, you'll eliminate unnecessary get-togethers and essential ones will be more productive. Both results are desirable.

You may have heard that committees should not be used to make decisions. Like all other generalizations, this is not always true. If you, as supervisor, can have your group of workers meet and come up with a course of action, to which most everyone, including you, agrees, then what harm comes from agreeing to take that action right at that time? None. Your workers may even properly interpret this as evidence that their views are appreciated and understood.

Some supervisors fear making decisions in meetings because it may reduce their authority in the eyes of their workers. This does not seem to happen if approached correctly. The workers may all agree as to what is to be done but it isn't going to be done unless and until you also agree. In American industry there is still a leader with responsibility in each group. As supervisor you are responsible for your unit. Whatever happens, you are looked to for an explanation by top management. Good or bad, you must accept that responsibility. Therefore, you must make the final decision on what is to be done, within the limits of the authority given to you in the organization. No one in a higher position in management is going to accept your explanation that all your workers thought it was a good idea, if the end result is disastrous. It will be your neck that gets chopped.

On the other hand, if all your workers all agree, and you don't—dig deeper. They may see something you haven't, or know something that you don't.

But if you believe you are right, then you can say, "I'm sorry, fellows, but since I have to bear the responsibility for decisions in this unit, we're going to have to follow my decision. I appreciate your views and have considered them carefully, but this is one time I have to disagree with you and do as I believe is right. Let's see what happens. If I'm wrong, you'll all have the right to tell me 'I told you so.'"

No reasonable person can take offense, or fail to cooperate, when asked to do so in a manner similar to the above.

Japanese total consensus has not yet been shown to be generally accepted in American business. The need for one person to be responsible at each level of operation is still the norm here.

American emphasis on a center of responsibility in team efforts has worked effectively over the years. Blending that with worker input before decisions are reached may be a refinement in our system which will bring even greater results in the future.

It's possible that the type of sports activities which have been most prominent in America for the past century may have greatly influenced business organization. Or at least, been used as a logical reason for organizing a business in the manner that's been used. All American men, and many women, will quickly accept that there must be a coach and a captain in a sports team. In football, there's no argument there can be but one quarterback on the field at one time. Someone must decide which play to use, and accept the responsibility. To accept this principle doesn't reduce input from any player as to circumstances or ideas which might help achieve the end result. With each responding with his best thoughts and observations from his point of view—his position—an analysis of what's good for the whole has to be decided by someone. It's this element of final decision and responsibility that has been accepted in sports—and probably has influenced business operations.

It is possible that the current emphasis on consensus— as appears to be Japan's special productivity quality at the moment—stems from at least some other factors, such as the attitude of the worker toward his company. A Japanese worker's belief that what he does, or doesn't do, will directly impact his company's results and therefore himself, may be far more significant than the manner in which his ideas are solicited. Also what impact so-called lifetime employment has is still uncertain. Cracks in this concept have also developed as increasing competition at home and abroad make maintenance of total payroll more difficult. Government assistance to business and the close cooperation that exists between these two bodies are also factors. The Japanese government apparently believes it is proper to see that business enterprises prosper and that maintaining that prosperity is good for the country, the government, and most of all, the people.

Trade union activity is reportedly much different in Japan as contrasted with the U. S. Unions appear to work for improvement in output, in the financial health of the employer, and exist in a spirit of cooperation with the employer rather than conflict. Evidence of the value to everyone in the cooperation of unions and business appears not only in Japan but in Germany.

In short, there is little need to destroy the American business organization structure in order to achieve improved productivity. Good management practices starting with good supervisory performance can improve American productivity to be competitive with any other system in the world.

Management must understand the proper use of capital and manpower in productivity. Providing the best tools to top notch workers who exist in an atmosphere from which they generate true motivation for accomplishment will bring top results.

CHAPTER 19 ———

"WRITE ME A REPORT (MEMO)"

This request can be as chilling as a cold shower to a beginning supervisor.

Occasionally, as a supervisor, you'll be asked to write a memorandum or report on something. Possibly an action that took place in your unit as it may relate to one of your workers, to a customer, or to someone outside your unit who may impact on you or your unit.

First rule: Don't be scared.

Very probably you have had little experience in formal-type writing. Don't worry. There is no real need for a separate writing style. The best business writing teachers say to write like you talk. Obviously, this is a generalization and some forms of speech—such as obscenity—may be used normally but it's not good to put those kinds of expressions into a written communication.

Here are a number of points to keep in mind as you prepare your memo or report:

1. Be brief. Whoever gets your communication has many other things to do besides read what you've written. He will be eternally grateful for a brief result which will use the minimum amount of his time.

   General George C. Marshall, chief of staff of all U. S. armed forces in World War II, was reputed to have had a rule that he would read no memorandum that exceeded half a page. If the momentous events involved in a global war can be reduced to a half page, anything required of you should certainly not need a lot more.

   Writing a short message is more difficult than writing a long one. A famous letter writer added a post script to a long letter he had written saying: P. S. Please excuse this long letter. I didn't have time to write a short one.

2. Be complete. Bring in all essential facts so that your reader will know everything needed to understand what you want to convey. Omit extraneous matter that adds nothing to the understanding of the document. Be ruthless in eliminating anything that is unnecessary. Be careful of the use of adjectives. They tend to reduce the impact of what you write, as well as reflect your feelings on a subject. Unless you are asked for your opinion on a matter, recite only the facts. Since your action or results were based on the facts as they existed, you have no need to be concerned about your reader wanting any implications of meaning from you. Sticking to only the facts will make the memo brief and crisp in appearance. Both decided advantages to you.

3. Be correct. Your spelling should be accurate—use the dictionary if you aren't sure. Use short paragraphs.

Short sentences. Short words. Your grammar should be correct. If your memorandum or report is sent to someone in higher management, you will be judged on all factors on the written page. It will be hard for the reader to know if you are reporting accurately on the events or facts given—but everyone in such a position will know proper spelling and proper grammar. If your paper contains these errors it could mean you are careless about the rest of the information as well. There's no need to take that chance on being misjudged.

Your education may not seem to you sufficient to be sure of spelling and grammar. Look around in your organization. There's always someone who knows what's right and what's wrong in these matters. Ask them to read what you've written and correct any mistakes. Nearly always, they'll be glad to help. It may even be that word of your desire to get spelling and grammar right will filter to other management people—to your benefit.

4. <u>Be helpful</u>. If you are simply asked to explain what happened, the above rules are all you need really to consider. On occasion, however, you may be asked to study some situation and make a recommendation as to what should be done. Some additional ideas in this circumstance may be worthwhile:

Use the proper addressing of your report which will usually be somewhat prescribed in your company. If not, simply put:

To: (Whoever should get the report or who asked you for it.)

From: You

Subject: (What is this about? Use just a word or two.)

Date:(Of this document.)

<u>Problem</u> (or Assignment)

Refer to 1 and 3 at end of chapter

<u>Recommendations</u>

As briefly as possible, set forth what you think should be done. If there is more than one thing, use numbers 1,2,3, etc. to show each one separately.

Refer to 2 & 3 at end of chapter

<u>Support</u>

Set forth key facts that led you to the recommendations. You may be as lengthy here as you think is important to the understanding and acceptance of your recommendations.

If there is much material you'd like to be sure the reader knows you've considered, put attachments to the memo using Exhibit 1, 2, 3, etc, keeping them separate in appropriate groups for better understanding.

Sign your full name,not your initials, at the end of the Support Section and before the Exhibits. Refer to the exhibits in the Support section. If there are a number of exhibits, list them on a page before they start, showing:

Exhibit 1— (Brief title)

Exhibit 2 —(Brief title) etc.

These aspects of memorandum and report writing can be applied to your personal contacts with other supervisors and higher management people. It's fun to talk about the recent football game, last night's date, etc., because in a business atmosphere, being friendly in all contacts is important—but the early concepts in this chapter will make you welcome in those places where people are busy. Always assume that everyone has more than enough work to keep very busy. Get to the point of your reason for contacting someone else, conclude your business, and then, if your time and the other person's permit, a friendly exchange of pleasantries can conclude the meeting.

Unfortunately, this process is usually reversed which often means that the business to be attended to is left to the last few minutes and sometimes is handled less effectively than it should be.

One slogan that will work well for you with busy people:

> Be Bright
> Be Brief
> Be Gone

As much as any other contact with people, the occasional meeting with another person on a business matter involves your being observant of the other person. Is he preoccupied, is he obviously pressed on some other matter, is he belligerent, is he involved in a telephone call, due at another meeting, etc. If these signs exist, reschedule your appointment until a more favorable time. He'll appreciate it and you'll get a better hearing later.

Always make an appointment to see someone else. Its courteous and will assure you that you can get an attentive hearing.

<u>Never</u> just drop in on another supervisor or higher management person with an important matter of business, unless it is an extreme emergency which the other person will recognize as such.

Further Explanation

1. The Doctrine of Completed Staff Work is a military concept of great value in business report writing. See Appendix 3.

2. You will want to separate some points from others and provide ready reference to them.

The most effective way is the use of numbers in an arrangement like the following:

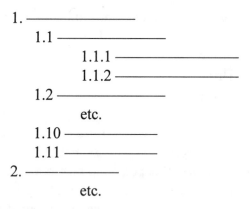

Use of letters, capitals, Roman numerals, parentheses, etc. is not recommended because the subsections get completely confusing.

In the system above, there is no limit to the subpoints that can be included—simply continue numbering in sequence as long as you need to.

3. Use side headings to separate the memo into appropriate sections.

CHAPTER 20 —————

SEND A LETTER

You may not be the literary type but in most supervisory positions, sooner or later, you're going to have to write a letter.

Your company may have a separate correspondence unit that will handle any inquiries, but if not, you may be expected to do so.

No panic. No really big deal.

You've undoubtedly written a letter to some one sometime on a business matter, so its not exactly your first letter.

There are a few simple rules that will help your letter writing:

1. Write as if you were talking to the reader. There is no such thing as a "letter-writing language." Years ago it was considered very sophisticated to adopt a style of writing that was supposed to be used in letter writing. Forget it.

Letters are to say something to the reader in a way that he can understand it. Using terminology that he will immediately understand is the best one to adopt.

2. Use a "You" attitude.

That means: thinking in terms of your reader rather than yourself.

A good rule is to try to start every letter with a "You." For instance:

Your letter of April 4 came today.

<u>NOT</u>

I have your letter of April 4.

3. Your reader is not interested in you or your problems. Like most people, he's interested in himself and his problems. Concentrate on solving his problem and he'll be grateful. Concentrate on yourself and your problems and he'll be angry, upset, or dissatisfied—depending on his feelings about his problem at the time he receives your letter.

4. Use short sentences. They read easier and keep you from being wordy.

But don't be curt. Remembering to use "please" and "thank you" often will soften the impact of short sentences.

Short sentences can make a letter appear choppy. If it seems that way to you, start an occasional sentence, or add a phrase, with a connective like "and", "but", "therefore", "however", etc. This is not a good practice to use constantly, but it can be occasionally useful.

Be aware of the inclination to string sentences together with "and" or some punctuation marks. Check your writing. If there are two sentences connected with "and", put a period before it, cross out the "and", and capitalize the next word making two sentences. Often, you will find the change made a distinct improvement.

5. Frequent paragraphing improves the appearance of a letter by relieving the image of a big black block of typing or handwriting. Don't worry unduly about what you may remember from school about paragraphing. Short paragraphs improve readability even though the strict grammatical content would be to keep the thoughts in one paragraph. This is an area where strict grammar rules may be bent in order to achieve other more important goals.

6. Always remember: your reader will judge you by the letter—that's all he has to go by. He'll also judge your company by your letter for the same reason

   The image your reader gets from your letter should be the one you wish him to get. Obviously, you'll want this image to be one that is favorable to you and your company—even if you are sending bad news to the reader. Maybe especially if you are sending bad news.

   Image is the main reason you must follow the accepted rules of grammar and society in your letters. Some people may not object to violating these rules but don't take a chance. Losing even one customer through a bad letter isn't necessary. Certainly it is not in your best interests or your company's.

7. Put good news first. If you are going to do what has been asked, say so immediately and then explain why. This order appeals to the reader. In many cases the answer is all he cares about. Your reasons are of no importance so long as he gets what he wants.

   For instance, SAY: The material you returned is indeed defective.

   NOT: While the returned material does not seem to be up to our usual standards, the basic dye lot had many problems.

8. If you have bad news, or cannot do what has been asked, build up to it throughout the letter and tell him that at the end. You want your reader to know of your explanation for your refusal, so he can understand it. If you put the bad news first, your reader may never read beyond that point. Your careful explanation of the reason for that answer will, therefore, be lost on him. Your letter will have failed to do what you wanted it to do.

9. Use of a subject at the top of a letter eliminates a lot of awkward references in the body of the letter.
   For example:

   Subject: Your letter of April 5, (Year)
      Claim number 23456

   Dear Mr. Jones:

   Thank you for your letter. You included the necessary information so your claim is being processed right now. You should have the answer within a week.

   Sincerely yours,

10. Tone is something you may have trouble with at first. It is the feeling your reader gets from your letter. The words you use and their arrangement create this tone. Use of words or phrases which cause irritation must be avoided. Certain words seem automatically to irritate people, such as: your error, you are wrong, alleged mistake, your fault, etc. Use, instead, soothing words and phrases to keep the tone pleasant and friendly, such as: appreciate, please, thank you,

our mistake, etc. Include the reader's name in the text, set off by commas, to help in creating a good tone. For example, You'll be interested to learn, Mr. Jones, that. . .

11. Avoid slang and obscene words. They are usually not descriptive of what you want to say, so it doesn't help your purpose. They may be offensive to the reader. Obscenities are totally undesirable in correspondence.

Make your letter clear, but concise. Long explanations may make you feel good because they cover everything involved. Be sure your reader needs to know everything you've written for him to have a clear understanding. Leave out what isn't needed for that understanding. Most letters are too long. People using dictation equipment and subscribing to the write-like-you-talk school often have lengthier letters than needed. It appears that letters were much shorter when they had to be handwritten. Actually writing the letter in longhand makes the writer try to say things in as few words as possible, to cut down the considerable time involved in handwritten letters. Abraham Lincoln's letters appear always to have been brief, but masterpieces in tone and clarity.

Do not talk down to your reader. If you can say to yourself after reading your letter that in any place you've implied a response of "You stupid" you've been talking down. Change it. This feeling of condescension is hard to see sometimes. Act as if you were the person receiving the letter. Would you feel upset by any of the words or the general feeling you have after reading the letter? If so, try rephrasing what you've written to eliminate what disturbs you.

Many letter writers complain that the hardest part of it is the close. This may be because they ignore an old rule: when you feel as if it is time to write the close, stop. You're already done!

A courteous phrase relating to the subject of the letter is a good way to end a letter.

For example:

    1. Let me know if you have any further problems.

    2. Thank you for writing. Your business is important to us.

    3. Call me if you have any questions.

There has been discussion for years on the format of letters. Elimination of the salutation and complementary close have often been proposed for business letters. At one time there was a national society dedicated to changing letter formats. Nevertheless, the bulk of business letters still follow the basic plan of "Dear Mr. - - -", and "Sincerely yours." You probably should too. Find out if your company has a preferred format, and if so, use that, of course. Otherwise, stick to the most common current practice of the salutation and close.

The inside address in business letters is there for ease in filing. It often seems a nuisance but in most cases is highly useful and therefore necessary to include.

Refer to the two sample letters at the end of this chapter that may help you as you begin your letter writing.

For your first few letters it is wise to ask someone whose judgment on this matter you would trust, to review your letter before it is sent to see if they think the letter is clear and courteous.

You can ask a knowledgeable secretary in your company to check the grammar and spelling so you will not be embarrassed by the letter or any unfortunate reaction to those elements by the reader.

Don't be afraid to ask for help on your letters. No one started in letter writing as an expert. Everyone had to learn sometime.

Also, most people are very willing to assist someone who earnestly desires to improve—in whatever activity they may be engaged.

(Your Company Letterhead)

April 17, (Year)

John S. Jones
Purchasing Agent
Ajax Company
175 Main Street
Anytown, NY 10101

Subject: Your letter of April 10, (Year)

Dear Mr. Jones:

Your letter caused a general review of our billing procedures to identify how a charge of $98.75 was added to your bill.

It appears that the $98.75 was a special reclinator you ordered on March 6. It was shipped to you on March 10. The receiving report showed delivery on March 11; accepted by a William Sonder on that date.

If you have any further questions, please let me know. Your business is appreciated.

Sincerely yours,

George C. Boddiger
Supervisor

(Your Company Letterhead)

April 17, (Year)

Mr. Amos Ursinger
6060 Dale Street
Anytown, CO 81064

Subject: Claim 7651
Your letter of April 10, (Year)
Our letter of March 7, (Year)

Dear Mr. Ursinger:

Your information sent to us in your letter has made it possible to complete most of the work on your claim.

We still, however, need the copy of the hospital bill as requested in our letter. As soon as this is received we can complete our review.

Thank you very much for your assistance.

Sincerely yours,

George C. Boddiger
Supervisor

CHAPTER 21

IMAGINATION, ATTITUDE, INITIATIVE, AND PERSISTENCE

<u>Imagination</u>

All of the problems of the world, including those of supervision, have been solved by people who applied their intellectual powers to the problem through developing creative, imaginative ways of eliminating the difficulty facing them.

Everyone has creative imagination. Many people, however, do not use it. Alex Osborn (See Appendix 8), a creative advertising genius, likens imagination to a key. "If you use it regularly," he said, "it will be bright and shiny. If you don't use it, it will become rusty, and eventually unable to work at all." Osborn also says that <u>everyone</u> has imagination. Think of the housewife who must plan the next meal. That is using imaginative powers!

If Mr. Osborn is correct, then every supervisor should

endeavor to use the powerful tool of creative imagination to solve his problems. If you don't think you have such ability, remember that everyone has it—you included. Start using it, and you'll be astonished that its effectiveness grows as you come up with an increasing flow of ideas.

Don't be too critical of your new ideas. No one's ideas are always good. Mr. Osborn once said, "You don't think up a good idea. You think up a hundred ideas and hope that one of them will be good." If that's how the expert works, then start creating ideas to solve your problems and keep on until you come across one that you believe will accomplish your objective.

With some practice, your imagination in creating solutions will increase. Use Brainstorming (See Appendix 9) to obtain ideas from your workers and other associates.

The real secret in this process is: write it down. Most of us cannot well remember a lot of different thoughts. We need the jogging provided by the written word. Don't believe you will remember all the ideas. You'll actually find that your memory is improved by the process of recording the ideas on paper.

One of my former associates, Fred M. Gregg, Jr., has a saying: "A short pencil is better than a long memory." Very wise.

In previous chapters, I've mentioned the need to use your imagination to create a solution to a problem. No book, no set of instructions, or no teacher can conceive of all the situations all supervisors may face at sometime in their career. Having an approach that helps you reach a creative solution to your immediate dilemma is more valuable than any other tool you can find. Use it.

Also, see Appendix 5 for a system of decision making used by Benjamin Franklin. It works.

Positive Attitude

Books, lectures, speeches, courses, magazines, sermons, and even religions, have been based on this common concept. You can read on the subject till your heart's content, and your eyes are exhausted.

No reading or listening will help you. You must decide.

Look at the favorable side of each situation by saying to yourself, "I want to help create a solution to this problem!" NOT: "Isn't this terrible. Nothing can be done."

Every problem is capable of solution. If it hasn't been solved yet, then there is more effort and imagination needed because it can be solved.

Creative solutions to problems are reached by your accepting the known fact that a solution IS possible. Now the task is to find it.

Regardless of how you have felt in the past, you can change your approach to a positive one by simply deciding in your mind that you will look for creative solutions and not for obstacles or objections to a solution. Grant Fitts, a former chairman of my company, issued a directive that no one was to use the word "problem". He said, "We have no problems here. Only opportunities!"

A number of interesting things happen when you make the decision to look for creative solutions:

1. Other people tend to respond favorably to you because they sense you are trying to reach a solution and are not trying to find reasons why something won't work or can't be done.
2. You'll mentally feel a lot better about yourself. You've removed the vinegar of a negative approach which in turn improves your own self-image and gives you a better feeling about yourself.
3. You'll find some solutions and be happy about them—and not be bothered by the problems you

haven't solved yet because you'll know that you have the capability to develop a solution.

You'll find some people who think this approach is ridiculous and will disparage it to you. Remember that all great thinkers and doers in the world have people running down their ideas and their work. Simply accept that there are such people, and then ignore them and their depressing atmosphere.

You may hear some one say, "That's Polly Annish. It's not the real world as it is." Baloney. You're not refusing to see the real problem. You're simply putting your energies on the solution. An old adage went: Keep your eye on the doughnut—and not on the hole.

Initiative

Initiative is taking action on your own. All the great ideas and positive attitude will never accomplish anything unless you take action.

Many people fear this step because of what may happen. "Something may go wrong. I'll be criticized if it fails, etc.

Of course you'll be criticized if your action does not accomplish what it should. Doing nothing when faced by a problem will get you the same result.

Initiative is required to make progress. Progress is made by doing something. Supervisors and everyone else achieve by taking the best action they can determine at the time.

Fear of failure is real and in many companies failure can be disastrous.

But nothing will be accomplished till somebody does something.

Be sure you have analyzed the problem as best you can, obtained any opinions you feel can be valuable or are required, then if you think you are right and have the authority—ACT.

Some helpful comments to still your fears can be remembered: A mistake is evidence someone tried to do something.

"They may be balls, or they may be strikes," famed baseball umpire Beans Reardon used to say, "but they ain't nothin' till I calls 'em!"

Humorist Robert Taylor of Waxahatchi, Texas, on hunting deer says, "In deer hunting, you have to pull the trigger—you can't aim a deer to death."

Action is the final step by a supervisor. To take it is your job. To do it with careful thought and consideration of all factors is essential. Once that is done, then results will only be accomplished by taking action.

Persistence

Calvin Coolidge was not known for his long speeches nor his lengthy writing but he made this masterful observation about persistence which is a universal truth:

> "Nothing in the world will take the place of persistence. Education will not. The world is full of educated derelicts. Genius will not. Unrewarded genius is almost a proverb. Determination and persistence are alone omnipotent. The slogan 'Press On' always has, and always will, solve the problems of the human race."

Keeping everlasting at it moves mountains. Nothing worthwhile has been accomplished without some difficulties. People who stop trying when confronted with obstacles usually accomplish little.

Persistence means trying different ideas to solve a problem when your last solution didn't work.

If you know your objective is correct, keep using your imagination and initiative to try different solutions.

The old slogan, "Winners never quit and quitters never

win" is true in all fields of endeavor today—as it always has been.

Being persistent does NOT mean being unwilling to accept changed circumstances. Persistency in trying to invent Saran-Wrap after someone else has invented it, is foolish. That is the time to try for improvement—your objective has to be adjusted.

Keep reviewing your objectives to be sure they are still correct, and if they are, then keep at it. If they aren't, rethink them and proceed in a revised direction, or stop if the problem no longer exists or someone else has solved it

The story is told that Mary Martin, the musical comedy star of *South Pacific*, as well as many other stage plays and movies, tried out for a chorus in a Broadway show when she first came to New York. After her performance, she was told, "Kid, go back home; get married; and forget about the stage. You have no talent."

Unwilling to accept this verdict, she persevered and succeeded!

APPENDICES

Appendix1

WHAT TO DO AND WHEN

Appendix 2

<u>Bosses and Leaders</u>
from *The Technique of Handling People*
by Donald A. Laird

Harry Selfridge was a Michigan farm boy. He started at the bottom with Marshall Field in Chicago. In ten years he was Mr. Field's partner. Later, he opened his own store in London and revolutionized English store methods. As H. Gordon Selfridge, he gave his staff in London this list of contrasts between bosses and leaders.

<u>The Boss</u>	<u>The Leader</u>
Drives his men.	Coaches his men.
Counts on authority	Gets their good will.
Keeps them guessing, fearful.	Arouses their enthusiasm.
Talks about "I"	Makes it "We"
Says "Get here on time."	Gets there ahead of time.
Finds blame for breakdowns.	Fixes the breakdown.
Knows how it is done.	Shows how it is done.
Makes work a drudgery.	Makes work a game.
Says "Go!"	Says, "Let's go!"

Appendix 3

COMPLETED STAFF WORK

Completed staff work is the study of a problem, and presentation of a solution, by a staff officer, in such form that all that remains to be done on the part of the head of the staff division, or the commander, is to indicate his approval or disapproval of the completed action. The words "completed action" are emphasized because the more difficult the problem is, the greater is the tendency to present the problem to the chief in piecemeal fashion. It is your duty as a staff officer to work out the details. You should not consult your chief in the determination of these details, no matter how perplexing they may be. You may and should consult other staff officers. The product, whether it involves the pronouncement of a new policy or affects an established one, should, when presented to the chief for approval or disapproval, be worked out in finished form.

The impulse which often comes to the inexperienced staff officer to ask the chief what to do, recurs more often when the problem is difficult. It is accompanied by a feeling of mental frustration. It is so easy to ask the chief what to do, and it appears so easy for him to answer. Resist that impulse! You will succumb to it only if you do not know your job. It is your job to advise your chief what he ought to do, not to ask him what you ought to do. He needs answers, not questions. Your job is to study, write, restudy, and rewrite until you have evolved a single proposed action—the best one of all you have considered.

The theory of completed staff work does not preclude a "rough draft" but the rough draft must not be a half-baked idea. It must be complete in every respect except that it lacks the requisite number of copies and need not be neat. But a rough draft must not be used as an excuse for shifting to the chief the burden of formulating the action.

The completed staff work theory may result in more work for the staff officer, but it results in more freedom for the chief. This is as it should be. Further, it accomplishes two things:

(1) The chief is protected from half-baked ideas, voluminous memoranda, and immature oral presentations.
(2) The staff officer who has a real idea to sell is enabled more readily to find a market.

When you have finished your "completed staff work" the final test is this:

If you were the chief, would you be willing to sign the paper you have prepared, and stake your professional reputation on its being right?

If the answer is in the negative, take it back and work it over, because it is not yet completed staff work.

Source: *The Management Review* June 1956 — Quotation attributed to Major General Archer L. Learch.

Appendix 4

"IF YOU WORK FOR A MAN . . ."

If you work for a man, in heaven's name, work for him. If he pays wages that supply you your bread and butter, work for him, speak well of him, think well of him, and stand by the institution he represents.

I think if I worked for a man, I would work for him. I would not work for him a part of his time, but all of his time. I would give an undivided service or none. If put to a pinch, an ounce of loyalty is worth a pound of cleverness.

If you must growl, condemn, and eternally find fault, why—resign your position and when you are on the outside, damn to your heart's content. But as long as you are a part of the institution do not condemn it. If you do, the first high wind that comes along will blow you away and probably you will never know why.

—Elbert Hubbard

Appendix 5

How To Make a Decision

"...I cannot, for want of sufficient premises, advise you <u>what</u> to determine, but if you please I will tell you <u>how</u>... My way is to divide half a sheet of paper by a line into two columns: writing over the one <u>Pro</u> and over the other <u>Con</u>. Then, during three or four days' consideration, I put down under the different heads short hints of the different motives, that at different times occur to me <u>for</u> or <u>against</u> the measure. When I have thus got them all together in one view, I endeavor to estimate the respective weights . . .(to) find at length where the balance lies . . . And, though the weight of reasons cannot be taken with the precision of algebraic quantities, yet, when each is thus considered, separately and comparatively, and the whole matter lies before me, I think I can judge better, and less liable to make a rash step; and in fact I have found great advantage for this kind of equation, in what may be called <u>moral</u> or <u>prudential algebra</u>..."

—A 1772 Letter from Benjamin Franklin to Joseph Priestly

Appendix 6

It's Not the Critic That Counts

It's not the critic that counts, not the man who points out how the strong man stumbled or whether the doer of deeds could have done them better.

The credit belongs to the man who is actually in the arena, whose face is marred by dust and sweat and blood, who strives valiantly, who errs, and often comes up short again and again.

Who knows the great enthusiasms, the great devotions and spends himself in a worthy cause. And who, if at best in the end, knows the triumph of higher treatment and high achievement. And who at worst, if he fails, at least fails while daring greatly so that his soul shall never be with those cold and timid ones who know neither victory nor defeat.

—Theodore Roosevelt

Appendix 7

Worth Remembering

How do people develop their attitudes and opinions? From experience, school, other people's opinions, newspapers, books, radio, TV, etc. A host of inputs received from many sources.

Many business leaders believe that short, meaningful statements, repeated or observed by workers, have an impact on their beliefs and actions.

Most famous of the thoughts used in business is Thomas J. Watson's THINK, found throughout IBM installations—a constant reminder that each person's creative powers are important.

Being aware of some of the great thoughts of the business world helps to identify occasions when they might be used to make a point with your workers or emphasize an attitude that will be beneficial to everyone.

Here are a few such observations that might be of value from time to time:

Most Important Words in the English Language

Three most important	I Love You
Two most important	Thank You
One most important	Please

Value of Trouble

All sunshine makes a desert.

—Old Arab Proverb

Character

A grinding wheel destroys glass but polishes diamonds.

—Old Russian Proverb

Self-Reliance

Every tub should stand on its own bottom.

—Old American Proverb

Memory

A short pencil is better than a long memory.

—Fred M. Gregg, Jr.

People

People are not books containing just a single page to be understood in one quick reading.

—John Jakes in *The Warriors*

Tact

Blowing a tune on your own horn that is pleasing to the ear of the listener.

—Old Saying

Terminations

Better an empty house than a poor tenant.

—Old Landlord Proverb

Obstructive Tactic (without appearing to oppose the project)

Always be in favor of the new church but disagree on the location.

—Gale E. Davis

Equipment

It's not whether the equipment is new or old, but how well it works.

—Richards D. Barger

Prejudice

Nothing is so painful as the sacrifice of a good healthy prejudice.

—Paul Hoffman

Education

Just because someone is not highly educated, don't make the mistake of thinking he is not smart.

—Ralph E. Heitmuller

Dissatisfaction

Progress in the world has always been made by those people
who are dissatisfied with the way things are, and strive
to improve them constructively.

Innovation

They copied all they could follow,
But they couldn't copy my mind,
And I left them sweating and stealing,
A year and a half behind.

—Rudyard Kipling in
Sir Anthony Gloster

Favors

He that has once done you a kindness will be more ready
to do you another, than he whom you yourself have obliged.
—*The Autobiography of
Benjamin Franklin*

Life

Life is a bed of roses.
Sometimes we're lying on the flowers.
And sometimes we're lying on the thorns.

Understanding

You can't reach objectives if you don't understand them.

You can't delegate anything effectively if you don't
understand it.

—Harold S. Geneen

Importance

Everybody wants to be a somebody. No body wants to be a nobody.
—Miles Schaefer

The Common Denominator of Success

The common denominator of success—the secret of success of every man who has ever been successful—lies in the fact that he formed the habit of doing things that failures don't like to do.

—Albert E. N. Gray

Credit

You can do a lot of good if you don't care who gets the credit.

—Frank L. Rowland

Desire

I am an inveterate reader of self-help books; and I have yet to find one in which I have a ghost of a chance.

—Carrol M. Shanks
President, Prudential
Insurance Company of America

Priorities

You're so busy mopping up the floor you don't have time to turn off the faucet. (Don't be so busy doing the urgent that you forget to do the important.)

Marriage

The secret of a successful marriage is to treat all disasters as incidents and no incident as a disaster.

—Source unknown

Action

Never complain. Always explain.

—Management Proverb

Old Russian Proverbs

—Not everyone with a long knife is a cook.
—If you're tired of a friend, lend him money.

—When you live close to the graveyard, you can't weep for everyone.

—Don't drive your horse with a whip—use the oat bag.

—James Reston
The New York Times
February 17, 1985

Leadership

A good leader inspires others with confidence in him; a great leader inspires them with confidence in themselves.

—Source unknown

Productivity

Productivity is the ultimate source of rising standards of living.

—Alan Greenspan

Nothing is less productive than to make more efficient that which should not be done at all.

—Peter Drucker

Appendix 8

Reading That Will Help You

Many of these books are old but their principles are sound and applicable today:

Acres of Diamonds. Russell Conwell, Harper and Brothers.

The Technique of Handling People. Donald A. Laird,Ph.D., McGraw-Hill.

How To Talk with People. Irving J. Lee, Harper and Brothers.

Your Creative Power: How to Use Imagination. Alex Osborn, Charles Scribner's Sons.

What an Executive Should Know About Himself. J. C. Penny, The Dartnell Corporation, Chicago.

How To Live 365 Days a Year. John A. Schindler,M. D.,Prentice-Hall.

12 Pointers That Lead to Promotion. Richard H. Moulton, Executive Development Press, Inc.

The Human Side of Enterprise Douglas McGregor, McGraw-Hill.

The Autobiography of Benjamin Franklin.(see Library or Book Store)

The Art of Readable Writing. Rudolph Flesch, Harper and Brothers.

How To Win Friends and Influence People. Dale Carnegie, Simon and Schuster.

Supervision of Women. Research Institute of America, New York.

The Power of Positive Thinking. Norman Vincent Peale, Prentice-Hall.

Touch Times Never Last, but Touch People Do. Robert H. Schuller, Bantam Books.

Management and the Worker. Fritz J. Roethlisberger, Harvard University Press, Cambridge, Mass.

A Message to Garcia. Elbert Hubbard. East Aurora, New York, The Roycroft Shop.

Think and Grow Rich. Napoleon Hill, Hawthorn Books, New York.

You Can Change the World. James Keller, M.M., Halcyon House, Garden City, New York.

Time Out for Mental Digestion. Robert Rawls, Executive Development Press, Inc.

Words To Live By. William Nichols,ed., Simon and Schuster.

Hand Book of Salary and Wage Systems. Angela M. Bowey,ed., Gower Press

What They Still Don't Teach At The Harvard Business School. Mark H. McCormack, Bantam Books.

Wages and Salaries. Tom Pupton and Angela Bowey, Gower Publishing Company, Ltd.

Appendix 9

Brainstorming

Devised by Alex Osborn of the advertising agency of Batton, Barton, Durstein, and Osborn, brainstorming is a procedure where a group is asked to suggest ideas for creating something new or revising something that exists.

The leader makes a list (preferably on a chalkboard or flip chart so all present can see) of all the ideas that are suggested by any member of the group, and its suggestor. Be sure the thought is clearly identified but without long explanations. You're looking for ideas, not a finished presentation.

During the brainstorming when suggested ideas are being recorded, there is an absolute rule that no one can object to any idea presented, however preposterous it may appear. There is to be NO JUDGMENT ABOUT QUALITY applied to any of the ideas proposed. It is this requirement which permits the process to work.

Often, outside of the brainstorming discipline, many new ideas are quickly rejected because someone says, "That won't work," or "What a stupid idea," or "We've tried that before and it doesn't work," or something similar. Anyone whose idea is greeted with such a response, or hears it used on someone else's idea, normally stops making any further suggestions because he will not be embarrassed—thus the reason for the brainstorming rule. You want every possible thought. The more ideas, the better.

Later, after thinking about the ideas, the leader marks the list with new numbers assigned to each item based on his belief of its importance—1 for the best, then 2, 3, etc. up to 10 (or as many as he thinks are practicable.)

Then begin investigation of the ideas, starting with the most likely one, completing its study before going on to the next most likely idea.

If the final solution adopted relates to a suggestion from the brainstorming session, compliment the suggestor before all the group. Brainstorming, handled this way, really works!

From: *Your Creative Power: How To Use Imagination*
Alex Osborn
Charles Scribner's Sons, NY